Performance
Intelligence
at Work

Performance Intelligence at Work

THE FIVE ESSENTIALS TO ACHIEVING THE MIND OF A CHAMPION

Julie Bell, Ph.D.
with Robin Pou

New York | Chicago | San Francisco | Lisbon | London
Madrid | Mexico City | Milan | New Delhi
San Juan | Seoul | Singapore
Sydney | Toronto

The **McGraw·Hill** Companies

Performance Intelligence™ is a trademark of The Mind of a Champion Publishing.

1 2 3 4 5 6 7 8 9 0 FGR / FGR 0 1 0 9

ISBN: 978-0-07-162514-2
MHID: 0-07-162514-3

This publication is designed to provide accurate and authoritative information in regard to the subject matter covered. It is sold with the understanding that the publisher is not engaged in rendering legal, accounting, or other professional service. If legal advice or other expert assistance is required, the services of a competent professional person should be sought.

—From a declaration of principles jointly adopted by a committee of the American Bar Association and a committee of publishers.

McGraw-Hill books are available at special quantity discounts to use as premiums and sales promotions, or for use in corporate training programs. To contact a representative please visit the Contact Us pages at www.mhprofessional.com.

To my home team: Nelson, Mary McCue, Myers Anne, and Lemuel Nelson. I will always be your biggest fan.

Contents

Foreword

When Julie told me she was writing a book, I was intrigued. She asked me if I would read the manuscript for *Performance Intelligence at Work: The Five Essentials to Achieving The Mind of a Champion*. She wanted me to consider writing the foreword. As her former professor it was an honor to be asked. I was eager to read what she had written. After many years in the field of sports psychology, I know there is great demand for solid material that helps one perform better. It has been the core of my teaching as well as Dr. Bell's professional pursuits.

After reading the manuscript, I was happy to oblige in writing the foreword. Dr. Julie, as she is known by her clients, has written a remarkable book. Sports psychology is not just for athletes anymore. For 15 years she has taken the principles of sport psychology and applied them to the business world.

In what I imagine is the first of many books about Performance Intelligence, she has coined the term that business professionals will adopt to assess how well they are thinking about their professional "game." Everyone wants a greater return on their investment in hard skills—what they are specifically trained to do. Said another way, for everyone who wants to perform better, Performance Intelligence comes alongside your hard skills and helps you perform your best when it matters most.

Performance Intelligence examines the thinking that accompanies those trained skills. At its core, Dr. Julie coaches you on increasing your Performance Intelligence. The five attributes of Performance Intelligence embody the elements of sports psychology that have helped many an athlete rise to elite performance status.

I have always believed that the principles that help athletes excel in sports can be applied to anyone seeking excellence. Julie has written a book that does just that. Performance Intelligence is the new standard by which we will measure our performances—professional and otherwise. When people think of maximizing performance, assessing one's Performance Intelligence will be essential.

DR. BOB ROTELLA

Preface

In writing this book, I focused on providing a general overview of the principle of Performance Intelligence. It is my hope that over the course of the 11 chapters I have succeeded, as Performance Intelligence can transform your performance in your professional and your personal life. As I was writing, I found myself reverting to a technique I have used for years in my coaching at the Mind of a Champion: storytelling. I think this is one of the most powerful ways of conveying information. It gives the listener or reader a way to invest in the experience that generates the teaching or coaching moment. In fact, this is how I learn. If I can relate to the story, I am more apt to hear it, ponder it, and incorporate its message in my day-to-day life. In these pages you will read about athletes and professionals I have worked with over the course of my career. In some cases, the names have been changed in the interest of confidentiality.

In my work with professionals, I have a particular passion for affecting leaders at all levels. I see how much responsibility they have for leading and managing teams.

Their ability to perform when it matters the most resonates with me because that is the end goal of Performance Intelligence. As part of this book, I wanted to speak directly to leaders in a way that would allow them to increase their Performance Intelligence. This will have a positive impact on their teams. Because this book focuses on leaders and will equip them with the tools offered in the chapters to come, I know that the impact of their adoption of Performance Intelligence will ripple throughout their organizations.

I have asked my colleague Robin Pou to help me speak directly to business leaders by writing a note at the end of each chapter. The information provided by Robin will continue to reinforce the principles of Performance Intelligence. You will enjoy his perspective as he has a unique blend of business experiences. Robin practiced corporate law in Texas and Silicon Valley before unleashing his entrepreneurial spirit. He began his second career as the owner-operator of start-up technology companies in a variety of sectors, including music companies, nonprofits, and the Internet. His experience leading people as the COO of several businesses, including an innovation strategy company that works with Global 1000 companies, has provided him with an up-close view of how business leaders can tap into their individual performance and influence their teams and organizations. Robin is committed to helping others implement Performance Intelligence and fulfill their unique purpose in business and in life. I know you will enjoy reading his input on Performance Intelligence.

Acknowledgments

For many years, people approached me after attending my programs and asked if I had written a book. I believed in the value of getting the content of those programs on paper but always cringed at the daunting book-writing process. I never knew where to start, and so I have many people to thank for the fact that you are holding this book.

Many thanks to Bob Rotella. Without his teaching and influence, I would not have developed the content needed to create this book. It is a special blessing to have him write the foreword.

I mention Jim Dawson in the introduction. His vision for the application of sports psychology to business launched my career. His commitment to Jesus Christ had an even greater impact. Thanks, Jim.

Of course, this book would not be in print without the team at The Dollins Group. Thank you to Dan, who contributed at every step of the way, from the first brainstorming meeting to the final document. His right hand,

LeeAnne, made sure every detail was checked off along the way. Claude offered the thumbs-up encouragement and gift of voluntary accountability. And to my writer Doug Hensley, who stayed in the game, even after that first meeting, thank you. High-five to all of you. You are a great team.

Much gratitude goes to the team at Storyline Networks headed up by Brad Edmonson and Jozef Nuyens, who have helped with the marketing vision for Performance Intelligence. Thanks for your partnership to ensure that more people will be introduced to content we believe in so firmly.

The Mind of a Champion team deserves many thanks. I owe a huge thank you to Sharla for bringing us all together. Thanks to Angela for contributing so much to our organization and to the book. But my real thank you to Angela is for inspiring me with your constant pursuit of improving your game.

Also with the Mind of a Champion is Robin Pou, my contributing author and coach. Thank you, Robin, for getting me so excited about this book that I had no choice but to write it. We could not have completed the book without your leadership throughout this project.

Captained by Nelson, my home team gets hugs. Although my children didn't really know what Mommy was doing on the "book-writing days," they supported me by being who they are. Their enthusiastic squeals and big bear hugs gave me the energy to keep going. Thanks, kiddos. And thank you, Nelson. Thanks for thinking *Performance Intelligence* was a worthy project. Thanks for your big smile when you shared the news about the McGraw-Hill contract with the family. Thanks for loving our family as Christ loved the church.

And finally, thanks to my Heavenly Father who makes the impossible possible.

"I can do everything through him who gives me strength." (Philippians 4:13)

DR. JULIE BELL

Dallas, Texas

Introduction

"Dr. Julie, it's Rick. I had a bad game last night. I'm not thinking right, but I can't remember what I am supposed to be thinking. Can you help me refocus my thinking?"

Rick had spent two years in a basketball slump. The two of us worked together to get him out of that slump, and he learned an even more important lesson: refocus quickly. If it takes some coaching to refocus your thoughts, just make the call.

"Doc, it's Jim. Do you have a minute?"

I always like hearing from Jim. He knows exactly when he needs coaching to maximize his confidence as he prepares for a sales call.

"Dr. Julie, it's Scott. I know this won't surprise you: We have more change coming. Everyone still has a job, but

our teams are shifting. Will you help me think through these changes for my team?"

I had been in a coaching relationship with Scott's team for just over a year. I knew that his team would continue to perform well during the transition. I also knew that it was important to ask the team, "What are you thinking?" so that we could focus during the transition.

Sports Psychology Meets Business Coaching

I'm Julie Bell. My educational background is in sports psychology. I founded an organization that is rooted in the principles of sports psychology. We take these principles to both the sports and the business worlds through the methodology we developed that we call Performance Intelligence. I love what I do and want to share it with you so that you can perform your best when it matters the most.

Before going any farther, I want to explain the difference between sports psychology and counseling or clinical psychology. Sports psychology is based on a healthy model rather than a medical model. In the sports psychology world, we assume you are mentally healthy. From that point we capitalize on your desire to improve your performance. Our approach helps you discover that you have another level to your game and teaches you how to get there. Doing that is a matter of recognizing where you are now and deliberately focusing on where you want to go.

The beauty of this approach is that all of us have the ability to recognize our thinking and then change that thinking to produce thoughts that set us up to succeed. Sports psychology is grounded in that precept. The process is easier for some than for others, but with the right desire and the proper coaching, anyone can change his or her thinking. Changed thinking leads to a change in people's actions to produce results that they desire.

Many people naturally think of sports such as golf, tennis, and gymnastics when they talk about training the mental part of one's game. I also work with athletes in team sports such as football, basketball, baseball, and hockey. Regardless of whether I have played a particular sport, I am able to learn the language. Is it called a game, a competition, or a meet? Is it called practice or training? In business, are they referred to as customers or clients? Do you have team members, staff members, or associates? At their core, the five attributes of Performance Intelligence are the same in both sports and business: focus, confidence, a winning game plan, self-discipline, and competitiveness.

When I completed my doctorate at the University of Virginia, I thought I would work solely with athletes. It is called sports psychology, after all. Thus, I began working with tennis players and golfers by conducting coaching seminars at country clubs. As it turned out, the amateur athletes in the audience were also business professionals.

They saw the parallel between what I was coaching and the business teams they "played" on all day, every day. This translated into many requests to coach people on business performance as well as sports performance. Thus was born the Mind of a Champion, my coaching organization.

My first client was Jim Dawson, who was CEO of Zebco at that time. He asked me to speak to his leadership team about Performance Intelligence. I warned him that I had never taken a business class and was unfamiliar with the ins and outs of business leadership. He told me not to worry about that. He was not hiring me to give the same canned-leadership, rah-rah speech heard time and time again. He wanted me to give a sports psychology presentation. He knew that the principles I taught athletes were the same ones that would help his team individually and collectively take their corporate game to the next level, perform well, and post a win for the business. He said he would teach me business concepts. He was right. My message resonated with his team members. Their performance improved, and I learned a thing or two about the corporate world.

After that first meeting, I joined Jim for a nine-month engagement as he became president of Brunswick Outdoor Recreation. At that time, Brunswick Outdoor was in an acquisition mode. Jim and I flew across the country from one newly acquired company to the next, talking to the employees and executives. Jim knew that those underperforming companies could improve—take their corporate game to the level Brunswick needed. Jim talked to them about their current state and the vision he had for their role in the expanded Brunswick corporate family. My goal was to coach them on how to reach the next level by helping them recognize their thinking about the acquisition. Once recognized, those thoughts could be refocused toward actions that would set them up to succeed in the tumult of the transition. The new actions allowed them to create new habits or routines that produced results consistent with Jim's vision and their goals. Routines in thinking set up routines in actions.

Although Jim has passed away, I cherish my time with him. Under his mentorship, I obtained an on-the-job MBA to complement my Ph.D. in sports psychology. I will be forever grateful for that. In return, Jim recognized that the best post acquisition strategy had to include changed thinking among the newly expanded roster of team leaders and associates. Jim understood the successful impact of training Performance Intelligence: It helps people perform their best when it matters the most.

As a result of my work with Zebco, it may not surprise you to learn that I also work with professional fishermen. When one of my anglers won the Bassmaster Classic, he credited much of his success to the work we did on his mental game. Afterward, my husband humorously asked, "What does talking to you have to do with his putting a fish on the end of that line, let alone winning a fishing tournament?" I explained that the sport of fishing is just like golf or basketball. If an angler is fishing one area of the lake in a tournament and becomes distracted by thinking he should be in another part of the lake, he isn't focused on each cast. He isn't confident with each cast. To win, he must have confidence that he is in the right area, on the right fish, with the right technique. Lack of focus and lower confidence unknowingly cause a change in his skill. He may not be putting the same action on the lure. Therefore, the lure isn't as appealing to the fish. He is not performing his best when it matters the most.

This same principle of Performance Intelligence applies to business. We all perform every day: in sports, in recreation, in business, in life. Confidence is confidence whether you are shooting a free throw, making a sales call, or leading a team. The attributes of Performance Intelligence stay the same across all areas.

Throughout the book I will reference stories from my experiences coaching athletes. I will show how using those stories as a backdrop sets the stage for the direct application of Performance Intelligence in business. The correlation is the same as that which was recognized by Jim at Brunswick. As it relates to Performance Intelligence, the worlds of sports and business are the same. You also will get a healthy dose of personal Dr. Julie stories. The reason I include them is to reinforce the idea that the principles cut across all areas of life. I believe in these principles and apply them to my own life as the wife of a pastor, a mother of three, and a business owner.

As you read the book, think beyond business leadership. Be open to developing the Mind of a Champion in all areas of your life. At the elite level in sports and in business, there are minimal differences in skill. Having the Mind of a Champion separates the occasional winners from the consistent champions. The lessons learned from top performers can be applied to everyone. That application allows you to develop the Mind of a Champion.

A few quick notes:

- Performance Intelligence is much more than positive thinking. It's about thinking in a larger sense. I will write a lot about what-to-do thinking. Some examples of what-to-do thinking are "Keep my head down" and "I will refocus after distractions." Examples of what-*not*-to-do thinking include "Don't hit the ball in the rough" and "I will not procrastinate."

- Performance Intelligence is about performing one's best when it matters the most. I use the word *performance* to describe any area of life you want to improve. You wouldn't naturally call leading a team meeting or parenting your three-year-old a performance, but I will use those examples in the book. Don't get hung up on the use of the word *performance*. Just think of an area of your life you want to improve or change and you can apply Performance Intelligence to get results.

- Performance Intelligence is not about evaluating every thought and every action of your day. Find the area you want to improve or change. That is the goal: targeting a specific area of your life. Performance Intelligence as outlined in the following pages will help you with that area, and the methodology will become ingrained naturally in other aspects of your life.

- Performance Intelligence is not for everyone. It resonates only with those who are at a point in life where they want to improve or make a change. If you want to take your game to the next level—whether on the sports field or on the corporate playing field—get ready to change your thinking.

Enjoy the game!

Performance
Intelligence
at Work

Your Mind Is Powerful

"Dr. Julie, it's Coach Smith. We have a problem. Robert is in a free throw slump. He is shooting 17 percent in games, yet he shoots 97 percent in practice. I know you can help him."

Robert and I met on the court later that day, and I asked him a handful of questions. What was the difference between games and practice? Did he forget how to shoot a free throw? Was he nervous about the crowd? Was he worried about his coach? Did the arena bother him? He kept answering, "No. That's not it." Then he did something interesting. He stepped up to the line, dribbled the ball, and said, "You know what, Dr. Julie? I think I'm jinxed from the line." I answered him simply: "Now we know your problem."

The only difference between practice and the games was his thinking. He thought about making the shot in practice. He expected his free throws to go in. In games, he thought, I'm jinxed from the line. And that thought changed his shooting percentage from the high 90s to below 20. It changed the execution of his skill.

Imagine a printout of your thoughts. What might it look like? If you saw that list, would it cause you to consider changing your thinking? Now put that printout of your thinking next to a list of the actions that result from those thoughts. Place them side by side and you will see how a change in your thinking can have a dramatic impact on your actions.

Three Principles of the Mind

Three basic principles of the mind guide my Performance Intelligence coaching. Let's start with the first principle.

Principle 1: Your Mind Is Powerful

Do you know that your mind is powerful? Think about a time when you had a nightmare. You might have awakened suddenly with cold sweats, a racing heart, or a fearful scream. Yet you were in bed—a warm, safe environment. There was no real danger, but your body reacted to your mind, to what you were thinking. Your mind tricked your body into having a real reaction to the perception of a fearful situation.

Here is an exercise that will demonstrate the power of your mind. Find a paper clip and about a foot of thread. Tie the thread to the end of your paper clip. (Now read these instructions in their entirety; then put down the book and do the exercise.)

Make sure the thread is tied to the end of the paper clip. Place the thread between the tips of your finger and your thumb with the paper clip dangling. It is important that the thread be at the tip of your finger and the tip of your thumb, not at the knuckle. Hold the thread gently. Without moving your hand or blowing on the string or the paper clip—only by thinking about it—move the paper clip from front to back. Just think front to back . . . front to back. Continue to think front to back.

Now, without moving your hand and only by thinking about it, change the direction of the paper clip. Move the paper clip from side to side by thinking side to side . . . side to side.

Next, without moving your hand and only by thinking about it, change the direction of the paper clip again. Move the paper clip in a circle. Repeat the thought in a circle . . . in a circle.

(Put the book down and do this exercise. You will be amazed at how powerful your mind is.)

What happened? Did the paper clip move in the direction of your thinking? I use this activity in the workshops

I lead. A majority of the participants are able to move the paper clip simply by thinking about it. There is no magic here. Your mind is powerful. As a result of your thinking, your mind sends out impulses all the time. Those impulses travel down your arm and out your fingertip and thumb, and down the thread to move the paper clip in the direction you are thinking. Congratulations. You now know that your mind is powerful.

To get an idea of how powerful the mind is, consider the story of the prisoner who was in a concentration camp for seven years. When he came out, he had shaved 20 strokes off his golf game. How? While locked away, he played every course he had ever set foot on in his mind. He would play one course a day, every day. The same thing happened with a Chinese pianist who improved under similarly trying circumstances. He was a gifted player before his incarceration, and he visualized playing each note of each song he had ever played. When he emerged, he performed at an amazingly higher level.

The second principle of the mind should be considered great news too.

Principle 2: You Control Your Mind

Do you agree? To know for sure, do this simple exercise. I want you to think of a song whose words you know. Sing a few lines of that song in your head.

Now I want you to sing the same song with the same words. Only this time, slow the song down.

Do it one more time. This time I want you to speed up the song. Make it go faster.

If you can speed up the song, slow down the song, or even change the words to the song, you are demonstrating that you control your mind. As easy as it is to speed up a song or slow it down, that is how easy it is to control your mind. Congratulations. You control your mind.

When you put these two principles together—(1) your mind is powerful and (2) you control your mind—you are ready to understand the third principle.

Principle 3: You Have a Choice in Every Situation

The choices you make in your thinking directly influence your actions. Here's another way to say it: Your thoughts lead to your actions.

The basketball player in the free throw slump at the beginning of this chapter was experiencing these three principles. Every time he heard the whistle and knew he was going to the line, he thought, *I'm jinxed from the line.* Those thoughts created tension, and that tension made it more difficult to make the shot.

These three principles are not exclusive to sports. Let's consider a business example. Your company has launched a customer service initiative. The company has invested a significant amount of money in training employees to handle difficult customers. The much anticipated customer surveys return, and nothing has changed. What happened? The focus of the training was on actions. No one addressed the thinking of the customer service representatives.

For example, let's say that one of those customer service reps has an upset caller on the line. That service rep has a choice in his thinking, and the choices he makes in his thinking will influence his actions directly. If he is thinking, This person is upset and wants to blame someone, how is he going to act? Most likely, he will approach the call defensively, frustrated, or listening for conflict.

Now take the same situation but change the thinking. This time the service rep is going to think, This person is upset and believes I can help. If those are his thoughts, what are his actions? Most likely he will approach the call in a helpful manner. He is listening for some sort of solution or pressing toward resolution.

Think about it. The person on the other end of the phone has not changed. She still is using the same colorful adjectives to describe her issue. She still has intensity in her voice. But the rep's new thoughts have led to his changed actions, leading to a completely different customer experience. Change your thinking and you can change your actions.

This book is designed to help you understand more fully that thoughts lead to actions and actions lead to results. In Chapter 2 we will take a deep look at the Three

Rs of Performance Intelligence. Knowing the Three Rs will help you change your thinking.

As an introduction to the Three Rs, you first must Recognize your thinking. Recognizing your thinking is a matter of using self-evaluation to identify your thoughts. It takes courage to recognize your thinking. Going back to the printout of your thoughts, would you want anyone to read what you say to yourself? Most people would say no. Why? Because we don't always have the best coaching voice for ourselves. Many times people talk to their dogs more nicely than they talk to themselves.

After you recognize your thinking, you will determine where to Refocus it. Refocusing is as simple as the service rep changing his thinking from "The customer wants to blame someone" to "The customer thinks I can help." For the basketball player, it was a little more challenging. Every time he thought about missing a free throw, he had to stop that memory and refocus on what he could have done differently to make the shot.

Once you recognize and refocus, you will need to create new habits of the mind, or Routines. Just as you have habits in your actions, you have habits in your thinking. Those thoughts create your actions and interactions. Many people, including me, see the flashing lights of a police car in the rearview mirror and experience an instant flood of adrenaline. Before your heart begins to race, you have a thought. That thought may be, What did I do wrong? That thought triggers the physical reaction. With the

Determined mindset outlined in Chapter 3, you can create new routines in your thinking that will lead to new actions and the desired results.

At this point you may be asking yourself, Does my thinking really matter in business? Absolutely. Whether I'm in a workshop with a group or doing individual coaching, I focus on thoughts that set up people for success and thoughts that set up people for failure.

I have worked with different groups within State Farm for more than 13 years. I find State Farm to be an amazing company. The tenure of its employees speaks volumes. If you have been with the company 15 years, you easily could be at the low end of the seniority ladder.

I remember working with many agents during a time of transition. State Farm had branched out from life, home, and auto insurance, and agents were expected to sell financial services. Some tenured agents had a limiting mindset. They experienced thoughts such as the following: There are professionals who do financial services. I sell insurance. I don't know how to do this. Those thoughts were setting them up for failure rather than setting them up for success.

My job was to help those agents refocus. As a State Farm customer, I clearly recognized that agents could provide financial services very successfully. New agents were having tremendous success because they wore a different set of glasses when they went into training. Their perspective was different. They viewed themselves as being in a relational business. I coached the tenured agents to change their mindset by talking about a couple of things.

First, I helped them change their thinking by giving them a different perspective. I shared a personal point of view. I couldn't wait for State Farm Bank to come to my state. This was a time when banks were changing their names every few weeks. It seemed as if my bank had changed names three times in a few months. I knew that State Farm had been around for a long time and was a stable force in our community. When the State Farm Bank came to town, I would be able to count on it always to be there for me.

Second, I talked about my relationship with my insurance agent. My agent knows what assets I value. My agent knows my current lifestyle and the lifestyle I desire in retirement. My agent knows everything I own. It makes sense that the person who already has all that information is in the best position to educate me on my investments.

I coached the tenured agents to think differently by realizing the value of the relationships they already had with their policyholders. I coached them on how their mindset had to shift from "How can I be successful at that?" to "No one else could do it better." As it relates to Performance Intelligence, financial planning is less about products than about knowing your clients and helping them make wise decisions. You can help your clients make wise decisions better when you have a relationship with them.

In working with the agents, I helped them recognize their limiting thinking. I coached them to refocus their thinking on the facts of the business. I also coached them to create new routines through self-discipline. Implementing the Three Rs helps drive the results you desire.

I was working in a one-on-one coaching relationship with a real estate agent. She wanted to grow her business and had a plan for doing that. She needed to reach out to a few "bigwigs" and ask for their business. The problem was that she suffered from call reluctance. During our coaching sessions, I asked her to describe her idea of bigwigs. She described them as some of her husband's friends and other important people who sat on different boards with her.

The tone of her voice telegraphed her thinking. She was intimidated by those so-called bigwigs because of their stature in the community. In helping her refocus her thoughts, I asked her to take the word *bigwig* out of her vocabulary and thus out of her thinking. I wanted her to describe her target market with different words and changed thinking. When she thought about John the bigwig, she was intimidated. She procrastinated by finding other things to do rather than picking up the phone and giving him a call. However, when she thought of her husband's friend John whom they regularly meet for dinner, she was able to pick up the phone and call him. That simple change in her thinking led to her most profitable year in business.

Whether you are in sales, service, or business leadership, you probably have experienced the obstacle of call reluctance. Let me share a personal example.

I constantly challenge myself on my thinking. I want to improve my thinking so that my actions will be aligned with my desired results. When I recognize that I am procrastinating about making a call, I ask my team to coach me through it.

My team asks me, "What are you thinking?" This is the crux of the issue. Once we recognize and refocus my thinking, we are able to prepare for the call. We think through the desired outcome. We set a course of action. We role-play. We answer the what-if questions to align my thinking and my actions with the desired outcome. When my mind is prepared, I am ready to make the call. Invariably, I find that the call is not as challenging as I feared. The discussion that follows is typically fruitful. My performance is in line with my preparation, and the results always seem to be beneficial for all involved. That doesn't mean I always get the business, but it does mean I learn from every situation. So can you.

Your thoughts before a call set you up for success or failure. Your thoughts after the call set you up for future success or failure. Let me play this out in terms of golf before wrapping up the call reluctance example.

The thoughts you have before your shot in golf will set you up for success or failure. "Don't hit the ball in the water" is a thought that sets you up for failure. You are focused on the water. You are thinking about what not to do. "This is a 7-iron to the back of the green where it will feed down to the cup" is a thought that sets you up for success. You choose a target, have confidence in your decision, and focus on what to do.

After your shot, the way you think about the execution of that shot will set you up for future success or failure. "Are you kidding me? I'm behind the green with a horrible lie and no chance of saving par here." These kinds of thoughts lead to tension and frustration. They do not set you up for future success. "Nice 7-iron. Good execution. Just a little too much club." Those kinds of thoughts allow you to learn from your game and keep your confidence high.

Let's go back to call reluctance. You made the call. You were organized in your thinking. You did not get the face-to-face appointment you were anticipating, but you did learn from the call. This customer is not a good fit for your services. You executed your skills well and had the Mind of a Champion, but it did not result in the desired outcome. You are not going to win every time even when you perform your best, but Performance Intelligence will keep you in the game so that you have a shot at winning your next game and the championship.

At this point, I hope you are thinking about your thinking. That is great. You are on your way to taking your game to the next level. When I speak about the next level, I am talking about performance at a higher level: greater consistency, better accuracy. Now let's discuss the Three Rs in depth.

BUSINESS LEADER HUDDLE

Did you do the paper clip exercise at the beginning of this chapter? If you did not, go back and do it. It is amazing. It highlights the idea that your mind is powerful. As a business leader, you probably already know this. You also know that you control your mind. If you are like me, it is nice to be reminded.

The key to this chapter for business leaders is the principle that you have a choice in every situation. The real choice is in your thinking. Earlier in my career, I wasn't always focused on the fact that I had a choice in every matter. In fact, I sometimes felt as if I were a victim of my professional circumstances.

In those situations I was missing the point entirely. I always have a choice in the way I think about my situation. This mistake could cause you to miss the Performance Intelligence opportunity.

Performance Intelligence tells you that you have another level to your game. You can change your thinking, which will lead to a change in your actions.

Here is the Performance Intelligence Challenge: Leaders, separate yourself from those who merely hold the title. Go beyond forcing a new behavior. Take the Performance Intelligence Challenge, go the next step, and evaluate your thinking.

2

The Rs³

"Doc, it's Terry. It's time to talk again. The playoffs are around the corner. The coach is looking at me to lead the team. It's now or never."

Terry was near the end of his career as a Central Hockey League goalie. I started coaching Terry when his teammates had so little confidence in him that they were leaving their positions to help him out. That created a bigger problem: So many people were in the way that he couldn't see the puck coming in.

I coached Terry to help him get his head back in the game. We talked about confidence with the goal of remembering how to be a strong leader on the ice. His team responded to his leadership. They were now in the playoffs.

Terry's "now or never" comment was a clue to coach him quickly. His old habit of creating pressure for himself was showing. He did not perform his best under that self-induced pressure. Terry knew this. That was why he wisely made the call.

At one time or another, all of us have received a challenging workplace assignment. It is up to us to figure out how to get it done. Do we execute? Can we execute? Or do we allow our brains to get in the way? It shouldn't seem like such a long way from the brain to the follow-through, but it's amazing what can happen to us within a few seconds.

Once we start thinking about a difficult task, whether it is pleasant or unpleasant, we begin contemplating the details, and too often we convince ourselves that we're the wrong person for the job, regardless of the reason. Before we know it, we're convinced there is no way to get it done. Our confidence is shot.

Our thoughts set us up for either success or failure, depending on our thinking. Perhaps you're a real estate agent who has just moved to a new city where the market is struggling. You might think to yourself, This is a tough market.

On the surface, that's not a positive or negative thought, but if you think about it, it is a thought that does not set you up for success. When you think about what a tough market it is, your next thought could begin, I will be lucky if . . .

You are already planning for failure.

At this point, it is time to change your thinking. Consider this formula for success: Your thoughts lead to actions. Your actions lead to results. I coach a three-step method that creates new habits in your thinking; Recognize, Refocus, and Routine.

Recognize Your Thinking

You first need to Recognize your thinking. It is difficult to change a thought pattern without first recognizing the need to change. Once you do that, you can refocus and create routines, which is another way of saying habits.

Recognizing your thinking means paying attention to those conversations in your head. The voice in your head is called self-talk. You will notice self-talk developing in children as young as age four. Ask a young child to count in her head the number of fingers you are holding up. You will see her head nodding as she counts off each of your fingers.

When my girls were four and five, the older one was very excited to tell me that she could talk in her head and no one could hear her. The excitement continued in the backseat of the car when she explained that concept to her younger sister. When her sister said that she wanted to hear, the older girl recommended putting their ears together to see if that would work. They *almost* understood the concept of self-talk.

You are the only person who can hear the voice in your head. Performance Intelligence is about training that voice to be a great coach for you. Listen to the voice in your head and then evaluate: I am thinking this. I wonder if this is a thought that sets me up for success or a thought that sets me up for failure.

I encourage people to write down thoughts as they are recognizing them so that they can review them and consider what they mean. For instance, one of our team members made a comment about keynote speaking: "Free talks lead to free talks." I believe that statement, and since I believe it, my default is to say no to an incoming call from someone who tells me that a particular organization doesn't have a budget for one of our Mind of a Champion (MOC) speakers.

That thought is not negative, but it could lead to missed opportunities. Thus, part of our winning game plan is that I now turn those calls over to a team member who is skilled at matching a client's needs with an MOC product. She doesn't have the thought that says that such a call leads to business not worth doing. Through her skills and strengths, she spends time talking to prospective clients, uncovering the clients' needs, and finding a budget that I was unlikely to imagine.

When she hears "no budget," she keeps exploring all the available options and having a conversation that my approach would have precluded. That may not sound like a positive or a negative, but the question is, Does it set you up for success or failure?

Here is another way of describing it: If you tell people at 10 a.m. that you're having a bad day, what does that set you up for? The truth is that you might have had a bad day until 10 a.m., but six hours of work remain that will be unpleasant because of the thoughts you're *choosing* to have.

The sports world is full of these kinds of examples. How many times have you read that a team can't win on the road or can't score in the red zone? If the team members believe such a thought, it sets up the team for failure. You may know the saying "Whether you think you can or you think you can't, you're right." That means that long-term success will elude you as long as your thinking is rooted in "I can't." You must begin by recognizing your thinking. Then you must refocus.

Refocus Your Thinking

When you refocus, you choose to think about something differently, preferably by coming up with a thought that sets you up to succeed. I sometimes get pushback that refocusing means lying to oneself. It does not mean that at all. You simply choose to turn your attention to another fact. For example, I was coaching a business owner who had a hard time getting up early and arriving at the office on time. When his alarm went off in the morning, he would think, I am not a morning person. I pointed out that after 20 years of thinking this way, it was not going to be any easier to get up the next day. I did not recommend that he wake up and say to himself, "I love the morning." That would be lying, not refocusing.

I did ask him to refocus on the facts. It's morning. The alarm is going off, and you are getting out of bed. You are simply stating a truth. Take the commentary out of the equation. That voice is saying things that set you up for failure. When you use this refocusing technique—focusing on the facts—who knows what you might find? Whether you actually become a morning person is irrelevant. Celebrate the recognized thinking, the refocusing of the thinking to produce actions that set you up to succeed.

In another coaching scenario, I was working with an NBA player who was struggling with his performance. When he talked about his years on a championship college team, he referred to the other players as his teammates. When he spoke about the players on his NBA team, he referred to them as his coworkers. I asked him when he started referring to his fellow players not as teammates but as coworkers. He said, "When I joined the NBA." I asked him when his performance slump began, and he answered, "When I joined the NBA." Something happened during the transition from college ball to the NBA.

I found out that the reason he called his teammates coworkers was that he did not approve of some of their off-court behavior. I gave him a homework assignment. He was to refocus his thoughts on the value each team member brought to the team. He returned with 14 pages of notes on each player's contribution to the team. That exercise allowed him to refocus during practice and games. This started to unlock his ability to perform his best when it counted.

Creating Routines

As a third and final step, it is time to create new routines in your thinking. Researchers say it takes 21 to 28 experiences to create a new habit such as going to the gym. A lot of people can and do go to the gym the first week in January, but the ones who are still there the last week of that month are the ones who are most likely to be there the following months.

Most people understand that you have habits in your actions. The true revelation is that those actions begin as habits in your thinking. Let's say someone has a habit in her thinking that tells her that she is not an effective presenter. Those thoughts lead to poor presentations, and poor presentations confirm her thinking. If that person approached her thinking differently, this is what it might sound like: I am being asked to do a presentation;

I must have something valuable to say. This would be the beginning of creating a new habit of thinking.

The old habit of thinking is focused on the mistake. The new habit of thinking comes when you play out a new experience in your brain. You know what happened, and you are familiar with the mistake. Now you know the correction, but you have to choose to focus on the correction to create the new habit.

Consider this example. I was standing in the kitchen with my older sister, and she told me that I was being overbearing; that was not a compliment. It would prompt me to say something clever such as "Oh, yeah," and we would argue. It was just a button she could push to get us into an argument. Ah, sisterhood.

What is the correction? Well, I told myself that the next time she said it, I would say, "Yes, it runs in the family." The next time we're standing in the kitchen, she makes the same statement, and I reply with the new comment I have been practicing in my head. She's caught off guard by my response. She looks at me funny, and then we laugh. It is an entirely different outcome. The key point is that I had to practice the refocused thinking in my mind before I could take the new action to make it happen. The next time it happened, I laughed about it instead of feeling insulted, and it's become a joke between us.

What I just provided is a simple look at Recognize, Refocus, and Routine. Avoid saying that something should have been, could have been, or would have been. Play out the experience in the present tense. Here is a mistake, here is the correction, and this is how I will experience it in a new way.

Take the following example. You're at work, and you need to have a corrective conversation with an associate. In the past, every time you've had one of those conversations with this person, it has not gone well. You've worried about it beforehand. You've never had a corrective conversation and then been able to go to lunch with that person. It is a strained relationship.

Continuing to think about this history into the upcoming corrective conversation will produce the same result. Right now, that is the habit of thinking you have and the only way you know how to do it. Think about taking that history and replaying it. For example, imagine yourself sitting in a conference room with this person, having a difficult conversation. Let's say it's confrontational in nature because it's about her inability to come to work on time. In your mind, you should be playing a film (a strategy that great teams use) to determine how you can interact better to get a different outcome. These films just happen to play in your head.

Old film: You begin the conversation about her tardiness. She immediately gets defensive. You focus on reacting to her defensiveness. Instead, see yourself playing it out differently. New film: She becomes defensive, and you use better listening skills. You ask for her side of the story and work together to create a solution. You have changed your skills so that when she becomes defensive, you do not become overbearing, and you listen better. At the end of the conversation, both of you are pleased with her commitment to come to work on time. By playing this conversation out in your mind, you understand that her actions may not change. You have changed your thinking about those actions and are able to create a believable scenario. You have practiced applying different skills in your mind and can take them into the next conversation.

Remember the basketball player in the free throw shooting slump? We addressed his thinking, and I gave him some homework. I asked him to go back through his memories and recall times he had made free throws. I wanted him to recognize those successes. After all, he was a college basketball player, and so he had to have made some free throws somewhere along the way. That was assignment number one.

His second assignment was to go through the recent history of the season and remember free throws he had not made. I had him start with five free throws he had missed. He was to correct them and create a new experience in his mind. If he was in a game against Kansas with two minutes left and was at the line and missed the shot, I wanted him to tell me what correction he needed to make. For instance, he said he needed to use his legs more on free throws at the end of a game because of fatigue.

I asked him what the new experience looked like, and he described himself in that game, standing at the line with two minutes remaining. He went through his preshot routine, thought about using his legs more, put the ball up, and in it went. He saw himself in that context and realized that if he had used his legs more to begin with, he would have made the original missed shot.

Instead of thinking about why he couldn't shoot a free throw, he began thinking about using his legs more at the end of the game. He corrected his mistakes and realized that he knew how to shoot free throws. Now, the next time he is in a game, he's playing with confidence rather than thinking about being jinxed at the line. Different thinking has created different actions, and that has led to different and better results.

Transfer that story to the business world.

Leaders need to go beyond merely addressing actions and coach their teams on thinking. If you have coached your supervisor on his issue of micromanaging to no avail, simply ask him what he is thinking. He may let you know that if he doesn't double-check his team members, he is afraid they will make a mistake. Talk to him about that thinking if you want his actions to change. Recognizing what your team members are thinking is a learned skill. It is not mind reading; it is a matter of understanding when to ask more questions to uncover someone's thinking.

I was coaching a successful pharmaceutical rep who was not picking up on the nonverbal cues that a physician had checked out of the conversation mentally. I knew she was someone who could pick up on those cues in social

settings. She had the skill. I asked her what she was thinking. She said, "I can't count it as a sales call if I don't get
through my whole sales pitch." You can easily coach a
person on that thinking.

It's easy to say, "I won't do that again next time." However, if you don't correct it in your brain, you replay those
tapes and create thinking habits you don't want. Recognize the mistake one time to see how to correct it. After
you recognize it, refocus on the correction. Then review
that correction until it becomes routine: a new habit of
the mind.

Recognize, Refocus, Routine: the Three 3 Rs necessary
for success.

BUSINESS LEADER HUDDLE

Poor results are the worst. Working hard for poor
results is tough. When faced with this situation, I
am cautious about telling the team members it will
be different next time. They will see right through
that. I don't want to go in the other direction and
focus solely on what went wrong. Although that is
important, a heavy dose of it kills motivation.

In Recognize, Refocus, and Routine, Performance
Intelligence provides the answer. Dissect poor
results to recognize the thinking. I have launched
many a project with a well-thought-out project plan

only to crash and burn. Invariably, in my traditional debrief, one teammate will make a statement that identifies the thinking problem. This often reveals a lack of commitment to the project or the plan at some level. This thinking often was linked to the failure of the project.

Performance Intelligence Challenge: Adopt a new way. As part of your project preparation, perhaps just before launch but in time to make changes, have your team members journal their thoughts about the project. Have them submit (maybe anonymously) those thoughts to you. This list of thoughts can be the subject of a discussion among the team members. Look at the listed thoughts. When a thought sets you up to succeed, match it to an action in your plan, showing how it can produce the results you want. When a thought does not set the project up to succeed, walk your team through the way the action coming from that thought would produce an undesired result. Coach your team to refocus the thought. That will lead to a discussion that improves the plan and achieves the successful outcome.

3

MIND

"*Dr. Julie, it's Kenyon. I won the tournament. The fishing was great. I would say it was perfect.*"

After hearing about Kenyon's success, I viewed some video footage of the tournament. Most professional fishing tournaments run three days, with each angler weighing in five fish each day. I was watching the film from the third day of Kenyon's fishing. On the fifth fish of the day—the winning catch—he set the hook, and it popped. The hook came out of the water and hooked him in the face. Kenyon removed the hook, threw it back out, caught another fish, and won the tournament.

In my mind, that was not a perfect day of fishing. Therefore, I called Kenyon and told him that, reminding him of the hook in the face. He laughed, saying, "Oh, yeah, I forgot about that." Before Kenyon and I started working together, one mistake would have pulled him out of his zone. With consistent coaching on trusting his talent and getting his brain out of the way, Kenyon was able to stay in the Natural mindset.

M stands for the Monkey on your back. The monkey on your back is the voice in your head that beats you up. It tells you everything that is going wrong, reminds you of everything that went wrong in the past, and predicts everything that may go wrong. Many of us fall into the trap of believing that everything that can go wrong will go wrong or did go wrong. By the end of the day, you could be driving home with a car full of monkeys.

The key, of course, is to recognize the monkey. I was coaching a lawyer who was fantastic at oral arguments but had a monkey on her back when she gave a presentation in front of her peers. The monkey would tell her everything that possibly could go wrong: "They will not think you are very smart. You don't know what you are talking about. You are unprepared. You have no credibility."

Can you remember a time when you had a similar experience? Did you perform better with the monkey on your back? A small percentage of the population would say yes, but most people would say they did not perform better. In fact, if you are like me, you lock down, have a shaky voice, or become distracted by the all-too-loud monkey talking in your ear.

Remember the third principle of the mind: You have a choice in your thinking. The choices you make in your thinking directly lead to your actions. If you have the monkey on your back, it is a choice. You choose either to keep it or to remove it.

One technique I use when coaching athletes is to train them to use a physical cue. I have them combine something physical with what they are doing in their thinking to make it more real. You might have seen this technique in action when a basketball player snapped a rubber band on his wrist to remind himself to have intensity on defense. You might have seen a golfer use a trigger for her preshot routine. The golfer might pull on her pants leg or touch her hat as a physical cue to get her mind focused on the upcoming shot. If there is a monkey on their backs, I coach people to look over their shoulders and say, "Get off my back." This act of recognizing their thoughts allows them to refocus on the desired outcome: What would you like to have happen?

Once I was coaching a group of distributors in a direct marketing company, a profession that prompts strong, specific stereotypes, possibly creating a monkey-on-your-back mentality among those who join those organizations. The thoughts might be something like this: Is it a legitimate business? or Will my friends stop taking my calls? or What will people think of me?

Refocusing those thoughts on the facts reveals a different story. These are the facts. This particular company has many positives. It markets a product called MonaVie, which is a high-antioxidant juice featuring 19 fruits. The premier fruit in the product is the Brazilian acai berry, which was featured twice on *Oprah*. Two ounces of the juice has the nutritional value of eating five servings of fruit. The "Active" form of the juice has glucosamine for joint lubrication and pain, and our society's population of citizens who need that increases daily. The company has a patent on processing the fruit so that a high percentage of the oxygen radical absorbance capacity (ORAC) is retained. The company was debt-free in only its second year of business. Also, it gives back to the locals in Brazil by building schools and other community projects. Armed with this information, the distributors began to think that this was the right product at the right time with the right company. They began to ask themselves why anyone would *not* get involved.

In my coaching, I always encourage people to find facts that allow them to move forward. This group of distributors knew the facts about the product. They loved the product and believed in the company. We had to refocus on facts about direct marketing.

We delved into some facts about direct marketing companies. Successful companies such as Pampered Chef and Mary Kay have been around for years. The essence of direct marketing is finding something you like and telling your friends about it. Many people do that every day. Whether it is a new restaurant in the neighborhood or the latest software download for an iPhone, we sell people on what inspires our passion. The difference with direct marketing is that a company will pay you for your referrals.

The real turning point for these distributors came when they refocused their thinking about the direct marketing arena. Their new, refocused thinking was that direct marketing is a legitimate business strategy taught at accredited universities across the country.

With this refocused thinking, the distributors moved from listening to the monkey on their backs related to participating in a direct marketing business to removing that monkey from their backs. That choice in their thinking allowed them to tell friends about a product and a business opportunity. Their passion about the product and the business opportunity came through in the phone calls, presentations, and follow-up. Simple changes in thinking allow changes in actions, leading to desired results.

Any monkey on your back can become an 800-pound gorilla quickly, but only with your permission. The way to overcome that is to work on your thinking purposefully and intentionally.

I stands for Intimidated, the next mindset we will discuss in this chapter. Intimidation occurs only with your acquiescence. Often, we overenlarge concepts or people, ignoring our personal strengths and resources.

A great scene in the basketball movie *Hoosiers* shows the team arriving in Indianapolis to compete for the state championship. The small-town kids from Hickory High look around that big gym, and you see a look of complete intimidation.

What happens next is a great example of what to do when you are intimidated: You go to the facts. How did the team react to that overwhelming situation? The coach, played by Gene Hackman, stacked one player on another and had them measure the height from the floor to the rim of the hoop. It was 10 feet. Then they measured the distance from the free throw line to the basket. It was 15 feet. They recognized that the court was the same as the ones they'd always played on. That thought refocused them, allowing them to return to their routines, thus defeating intimidation.

In business, you may be intimidated by Mondays. Sunday afternoon we start thinking about Monday: work that awaits us, inevitable distractions, meetings, competition with colleagues who might have worked over the weekend. Work looms so large that one can't help being intimidated by the days ahead. Instead of falling into the trap of the Intimidated mindset by artificially building up a client, a marketplace, or even a day such as Monday, refocus on your skills and talents.

I work with a lot of junior tennis players. In an effort to be helpful, parents will research a child's upcoming opponent. They will learn the opponent's number of wins, ranking, and strengths. Ironically, rather than this information being helpful, many players spend more time focusing on their opponents and building them up in their minds than they do focusing on their own skills. Unfortunately, when they walk out on the court for the much-anticipated match, those players tend to be down a set before the first serve.

Another example comes from youth soccer. Many children younger than age 10 believe that anyone taller or older is guaranteed to win. This physical advantage creates the perception in the player that the older or larger opponent should win. All too often, one can carry this assumption into adulthood. The problem is that it is faulty. Have you ever ceded mental victory to someone with a nicer car or a higher income or a higher-profile job? If competitors have a higher level of education, you may assume erroneously that they have more credibility. The damage occurs when you build up obstacles and people rather than focusing on your skills, strengths, and resources.

I worked with a golfer who aspired to be on the PGA tour; his short game was his strength. He rated it a 6 on a scale of 1 to 10. I asked him what a 10 would look like. He said that professionals hole out (sink the ball in the cup) 9 out of 10 shots when they are 100 yards from the green. I asked, "When was the last time you saw that?" He was unable to support his belief with a specific example. It just doesn't happen. However, he had mentally built up professional golfers to such an extent that he ignored the strength of his own short game. When you believe something that deeply in your mind, it keeps you from performing your best when it matters the most. We all have some of these flawed beliefs. You could be a pharmaceutical rep who is intimidated by the top physician in the area or a manager trying to give a presentation with her boss in the room.

Again, the only way to be intimidated is to choose to build up other things or other people mentally. This can paralyze your instincts, leading to actions that create undesired results. Recognizing that you can choose not to be intimidated makes all the difference.

N stands for the third mindset: the Natural mindset. You may have heard an athlete talk about being in the zone or having a peak performance. You may have experienced being in the zone. Typically, people describe it as fun and easy. It makes the performance seem effortless.

When people are in the Natural mindset, they are doing what they are trained to do. You are in the Natural mindset when you write your signature. You are well trained and trust that training. If you think too hard when writing your signature, it looks unnatural. If you want to be in the Natural mindset, you must be well trained and keep your skills sharp so that you can trust that training.

In the opening story, Kenyon was in the Natural mindset. He wasn't thinking too hard. He found his fish in the prefish days. He created a plan. Then he trusted his talent.

Unfortunately, researchers on peak performance tell us that people are in the natural mindset only about 10 percent of the time. We live in a culture that can prompt overthinking. Every time we have to think intentionally about what we are doing, we are pulled out of that natural, trusting mindset. Whenever you experience change, you have to think about what you are doing. When was the last time you moved into a new residence? Moving can be very stressful because everything is changing. You have to think about everything you are doing. Your light switch is not in the same place. You have to think about where to find your toothbrush, your socks, and your dishes. You cannot be in your Natural mindset.

The good news is that you can train yourself to be in the Natural mindset more often through determination.

D is the Determined mindset that occurs when you make a conscious choice to focus on a solution or correction rather than worrying about problems or mistakes. When people are in the Determined mindset, they practice intentional thinking.

Do this exercise: Clasp your hands together with your fingers interlocked. Is the right thumb or the left thumb on top? Shake out your hands by your side and clasp them together again. The same thumb is on top, right? You can do this with your eyes closed. You can do it with your hands clasped behind your back, and the same thumb will always be on top because you are well trained. You are in the Natural mindset. Now clasp your hands together with the other thumb on top. It feels uncomfortable, doesn't it? That is the case because it is not natural. But you can do it. You have to think intentionally about what you are doing, but you can do it. Believe it or not, if you do it often enough, it actually becomes natural. You can train yourself to develop a new routine.

This takes place in the performance training center, where we focus on corrections and solutions that can move you from the Determined mindset into the Natural mindset more often. Training allows you to avoid shifting into panic mode when—not if—a crisis occurs. People in the Determined mindset go straight to solutions; that is why they are so successful.

The golf movie *Tin Cup*, starring Kevin Costner, offers a great illustration of the MIND concept. Costner is out on the driving range trying to hit the ball, and every shot veers off dangerously toward others on the range. He looks at his caddy, played by Cheech Marin, and asks, "What am I doing wrong?"

That is the wrong question. He is focused totally on his mistakes. His caddy has him go through a series of seemingly silly antics that preoccupy him and keep him from thinking about his swing. What happens next? He steps up to the ball and hits a perfect 7-iron. Looking at his caddy, Costner wonders how he did it. At that moment, I would say he was in the Natural mindset. He wasn't thinking. He was doing what he was trained to do. He had gotten his brain out of the way.

Performing your best when it matters the most is an intentional choice. It really is all in your MIND.

BUSINESS LEADER HUDDLE

Dr. Julie advocates journaling. I do too. If one of the elements of the methodology of Performance Intelligence is to recognize your thinking, how can you do this without journaling on some level, either verbally or in writing? The premise of the book is that Performance Intelligence resonates with people who want to improve, and so I am assuming you are taking the doctor's advice.

Once you've journaled your thoughts, categorize them into the four mindsets. How often are you in the Monkey on your back, Intimidated, Natural, and Determined mindsets over the course of a day? Look at the actions that resulted from those thoughts. How does the time you spend in each mindset affect your performance?

Many people, even leaders, recognize the monkey on their backs. Why is that? Leaders can be harder on themselves than anyone else can. A leader's boss likes this. He doesn't have to beat the leader up for his or her mistake. The leader already has done that.

The journaling exercise typically reveals that leaders do not spend as much time in the Monkey on your back mentality as they think. In fact, they spend more time in the Determined and Natural mindsets. This is as it should be. Knowing this fact makes all the difference in how you think about your day. If you find that you are spending too much time with the monkey on your back, recognizing that will allow you to refocus your thoughts on those which set you up to succeed.

Performance Intelligence Challenge: Be an effective leader by coaching the Determined mindset in your team. When you hear the monkey, comment about it. Simple coaching comments such as "Do you really think that?" will open a dialogue and take your team to the next level.

4

What Is Performance Intelligence?

"Dr. Julie, it's Sarah. I did my homework assignment. I took notes while I watched my videos, and I read them after the tape was over. I discovered I was more successful than I ever gave myself credit for in the past. After I was all done reviewing and making notes, I wrote this at the bottom of the page: 'I was always successful, and I'm really good at this!' You have taught me about performing my best when it matters most on the rodeo circuit. I will take these lessons into every area of my life."

Sarah was right. Performance Intelligence is not just for athletes or corporate athletes. Learn the lessons and apply them every time you want to improve or change.

Have you ever stood on a putting green and made putt after putt? No matter where you line up, the ball is going in the cup. Same thing when you practice free throws. Dribble, dribble, dribble. Look, shoot—swish.

Nothing to it, right? Now accomplish one of these seemingly routine tasks when it matters the most. It's an entirely different experience stepping onto the eighteenth green with a one-shot lead in the tournament and nine feet between your ball and the cup. It's a different experience when you step up to the free throw line in a tie game with two seconds left and 10,000 people cheering against you so that their team can win the championship.

This is where Performance Intelligence comes into play, and it's a concept that works whether you are in a sports stadium or a business arena.

Simply put, Performance Intelligence is the ability to perform your best when it matters the most. It says you have another level to your game. Can you use your strengths, talents, skills, and resources at the right time, in the right place, and with the right form?

Many people can perform best when the economy is great and a logo is all that is needed to grow the business. But what happens when those variables turn against you—when the economy is tight, unemployment is high, the stock market is plunging, and your competition is gaining market share?

I have found that people can perform well when they do not perceive a situation to be pressure-packed, for example, in practice and day-to-day routines. When the situation is natural, their performance flows.

Our aim at the Mind of a Champion is to enlarge the pool of people who can perform their best in adversity, sustaining and steering their organizations through a challenging climate. Performance Intelligence follows a healthy model to improve performance in a specific area.

In the professional world, Performance Intelligence starts with certain questions: Where are you now? Where do you want to go? How are you going to get there?

Everyone wants an edge. After buying new equipment and taking lessons, a person may decide to see a sports psychologist. In the business world, you hire the right people and invest money in leadership development, but you may reach a point where everyone is on a level playing field. You want an edge. The edge comes from getting people to think differently.

This is different from executive coaching, which generally involves a one-on-one setting. Although Performance Intelligence training can be implemented in a one-on-one manner (coaching), it also can take place with a group (keynotes and workshops). Many executive coaches focus on technique: Do x to gain y results. Performance Intelligence is complementary to executive coaching because it addresses the thinking behind the techniques.

I have a friend in sales whose executive coach advised her about how many calls to make per day. The coaching was business plan–oriented, aimed primarily at enhancing technique. Performance Intelligence coaching contends that you may have a game plan, but if you are not executing it, there is a reason. That reason is your thinking. Performance Intelligence is all about your thinking.

I was coaching a client who was working with a consultant on a business plan. I think business plans are wonderful, but you must make sure your plan reflects your thinking. It's been my experience that you can spend months writing a business plan, shake hands when the final document has been written, walk out of the conference room, and know exactly what is in the plan that you have doubts about. But no one ever talks about those thoughts. You must address those thoughts to guarantee that your business plan becomes a winning game plan.

Imagine my client's conference room. All these people are sitting around the room. They all have different skill sets. Each will hear the conversation a certain way. I listen for expressions of doubt such as "We'll probably do this." If you say "probably," it means you are less than 100 percent confident that you will do it. You have doubt in your language. What you say gives insights into your thinking.

I was leading a two-day workshop for a floral company. The morning of the second day, I took a full pitcher of water. As I was about to pour, I sarcastically said, "Watch me spill this water." In unison, those around the table held me accountable in the terms I use in my coaching by saying, "If you think that way, you really will spill it." I put the pitcher down and said, "Welcome to my world." After refocusing my thinking, I successfully poured a tall glass of water. I talk about these principles all the time, and I still have to be held accountable to my thinking. Performance Intelligence is for everyone.

Is your performance the same when it's just you practicing as it is when the stakes are real? Can you deliver the same winning presentation when you are practicing in the room alone and when you are in front of an important client with your boss in the room?

People often see their performance change when they perceive that pressure exists or when the environment does not seem conducive to performing at their best. Regardless, Performance Intelligence strengthens your ability to understand a situation and its conditions and still perform your best.

I was participating in a corporate retreat as the keynote speaker. In one of the meetings, 20 people were discussing their current marketing campaign. The conversation very quickly turned negative. People talked about how this campaign was no different from previous efforts. Personally, I loved the campaign, and I was a part of the demographic they were trying to reach.

The people in that room were leaders who not only had to understand and embrace the campaign but also had to turn around and sell it internally to those at the next level. I remember thinking that if they were displaying this lack of commitment to the campaign, there was no way they would be able to make the sale.

What does that have to do with Performance Intelligence? Can you perform your best when you know your organization's marketing campaign is not what you want it to be? It becomes a matter of refocusing on the steps you will take to make the campaign work. Think about using the Determined mindset and taking a proactive approach. It's considerably more productive than sitting back and picking apart the campaign because it fails to meet your expectations.

I coached them to take personal responsibility for figuring out why someone at their corporate office decided that this was a good marketing campaign. They had to put themselves in the shoes of those marketing folks. The goal was for them to find the facts that resulted in the campaign. I directed them to do it before they left the room that day.

This example is about a successful company that employs many smart people. This is not a company that would randomly ask someone in the hallway for an idea and then spend millions of dollars on it. The company's leaders take reasoned approaches and employ thoughtful methods before making such vital, expensive decisions. I knew this to be fact because of the organization's success and my tenure with it as a coach.

Since the organization does nothing simply on the basis of happenstance, I told the members of the group that if they couldn't figure it out, they needed to make a phone call to someone at the corporate office for help. The bottom line was that they had to look at that campaign, connect with some aspect of it, and then make it work with the people in their reporting line. It was a matter of self-discipline and a Determined mindset.

Companies see many initiatives fail not because they stem from bad ideas; they fail because people don't get on board 100 percent. Too often, people want to see if something will work for other people first. That wait-and-see mentality does not get you to perform your best when it matters the most. It is the reason your efforts fail.

Look at this from the perspective of football. The offense huddles up, and the quarterback calls a play. One of the offensive linemen decides to wait and see if the play will work. As it turns out, it does not work. The reality is that because the lineman failed to do his job, he is the reason the play didn't work.

I have worked with organizations in which fantastic initiatives went down the drain because people did not take personal responsibility and say, "This is why we're doing this, it makes sense for our organization, and I'm going to support it a hundred percent."

For example, I was working with a pharmaceutical company that spent millions of dollars launching a drug in the marketplace only to see the drug cause some negative interactions, forcing it to be pulled off the shelves. I coached the company representatives on a plan to go into physicians' offices across the country with confidence. Of course, some representatives wondered how they could do that. My answer: "How can you afford not to address the issue this way?" Look at the integrity of the company, which cared more about the health of its patients than about the millions of dollars it invested in the drug. With that refocused thinking, the representatives were able to engage the doctors with complete confidence and communicate that integrity. That is how you build and grow relationships. The representatives understood what happened and why it happened and believed in the company's reason for withdrawing the product. They knew the pharmaceutical company was thinking about how the decision would affect everyone.

How do you raise your team's performance to this level? Performance Intelligence is made up of five attributes. Although I devote an entire chapter to each attribute, I want to provide an early overview to familiarize you with the terminology.

Focus

Everyone knows how to focus, but at times people just don't know where to focus. In Chapter 5, you will learn to have a singular focus by focusing on playing to win versus playing not to lose and by focusing on past mistakes.

In this multitasking world, why would anyone want to have a singular focus? We can learn a great lesson about focus from the lion tamer at the Barnum & Bailey

Circus. He would enter the ring with a gun on his side, a whip in one hand, and a stool in the other hand. When asked which he would choose if he could take only one of the three items into the ring, he said he would take the stool. If he put the four-legged stool in the lion's face, the lion would freeze and seem to be paralyzed. A lion cannot attack if it cannot focus, becoming distracted and disoriented.

Many things compete for a person's focus in a multitasking world. Performing one's best when it matters the most takes a singular focus. You can multitask, but for each additional task you take on, your attention diminishes and your focus decreases. You lose effectiveness.

Too often, we focus on what we don't want to have happen rather than where we are going and how we will get there. Focus is a matter of paying attention to what is most necessary at the right time. This doesn't mean that the distractions go away. It means that you are in control of your focus.

Although top performers make mistakes, they remain top performers because they can focus past a mistake. When you do this, you are focused on the correction. The correction requires you to identify information on what to do, leading to a greater probability of that happening in a similar situation.

I find that great athletes focus on playing to win rather than playing not to lose. Playing not to lose is tentative. It is defensive. It involves protecting what you have rather than creating what you want. On the other side, playing to win is all about pursuit of the goal. It is motivating. It is playing out your vision. It is proactive. When you are focused on playing, the win takes care of itself.

Confidence

Confidence influences everything people do. Two common mistakes people make are (1) being confident in the outcome rather than confident in the process that creates the outcome and (2) having all-or-nothing confidence. The great news is that confidence can be trained.

In most cases, you cannot be 100 percent confident in the outcome because you do not have complete control of all the variables. Instead of being confident in the outcome, we will look at being confident in the process that creates the outcome. This way of thinking will allow you to be confident today and be confident about achieving future goals.

Almost everyone has a history of success. When we approach confidence from an all-or-nothing perspective, we don't take full advantage of the confidence we already own. In Chapter 6, we will recommend taking whatever project or task you are working on and breaking it down to its basic components and identifying specific, necessary skills. Then we will use your history of successful experiences with those skills to build your confidence one step at a time.

Every thought you have can make you more confident or more doubtful. To train your confidence methodically, you have to recognize success on a daily basis. After introducing you to the topic of confidence, this book will teach you how to define success and failure accurately (Chapter 7). With the new mindset, you will be more adept at recognizing success on a daily basis. Every success you have gives you a reason to be confident.

Winning Game Plan

A winning game plan, which is more than a mere game plan, will define your win. It will allow you to look at what's working and what's not working. In Chapter 8, we will look at executing a winning game plan with confidence.

Not everyone defines a win the same way. I have found that some athletes strive to have the fastest time among the competition and others are focused on a personal best. Motivation varies in business as well. Money motivates some people. Others find motivation through time off or praise. Your winning game plan begins with your personal definition of success.

When I begin coaching individuals or teams on a winning game plan, they invariably want to talk about what is not working. Your winning game plan will start by examining what is working. The aspects that work in your life—those things that create current successes—are the building blocks of your wining game plan.

A winning game plan is not about seeing things through rose-colored glasses. We will take a look at what isn't working too. We do this by recognizing undesirable results. We will reverse-engineer the concept "Thoughts lead to actions, and actions lead to results." We will look at the actions that created the results. Then we will take one more step: We will scrutinize the thinking behind the actions that led to undesirable results.

After you create a winning game plan, you must execute it. When you are confident in your winning game plan, you will understand the benefit of rewarding yourself upon its execution rather than waiting for the numbers or other measures to indicate that it's time to give yourself a reward. If this makes you nervous, you may have only a game plan, not a winning game plan.

Self-Discipline

Self-discipline is twofold. It begins with this statement: I desire to improve or change. After that declaration, self-discipline involves voluntary accountability, which sets the stage for real coaching.

The number of people who say they want to lose weight is staggering compared with the number of people who actually do anything about it. The same is true in a business culture. If you ask people in an organization if they want to move their performance to the next level, you will hear a resounding yes. You may even see a majority of those people going to classes to improve their skills. But how many are willing to make a mistake and go to their supervisor or manager and say, "I messed up. Will you coach me through it?" That is real Performance Intelligence coaching. Without self-discipline, coaching can be seen as being sent to the principal's office. The self-discipline that is part of Performance Intelligence involves voluntary accountability: unlocking the coach within you. The lower your self-discipline; the higher your need for voluntary accountability.

Competitiveness

To perform your best when it matters the most, you have to have an internal desire to win. Most people think about this as competing against others. What does this look like? If I win, you lose. Or, even worse, if you win, I lose. Competitiveness as an attribute of Performance Intelligence recasts the win-lose relationship. To raise your performance to a higher level, you have to start looking for win-win scenarios. You also have to compete against yourself. We coach you to say, "My competitiveness is about taking my game to the next level rather than simply beating you."

Once you understand the impact that training the attributes of Performance Intelligence will have on your game, you will need tools to train. Chapter 11,

"Performance Training Center," will equip you to perform your best when it matters the most.

BUSINESS LEADER HUDDLE

When I talk casually to business leaders about the concept of Performance Intelligence, I don't always have the opportunity to hand them this book. I have to give them the elevator pitch, or the shortened version, and this is what I say to them.

Performance Intelligence seeks to increase the number of people who perform their best when it matters the most. When everything is going well, a large number of people can excel. But when the tide turns, who can still make it happen? When the economy is bad, your competition has toughened, or other variables that you do not control go south, who can win? The number of people shrinks, right? Why is that?

Think about Tiger Woods and his closest competitor in any particular year. Tiger almost always wins. His competition sometimes wins. What is the difference? You've seen Tiger win against all odds. Tiger has seen tough times. Yet he wins more often than not. Some might say he is more skilled. Maybe. I tend to think that he has mastered the **MIND.**

Performance Intelligence Challenge: Economic hard times that sometimes lead to difficult personal times can keep even the best man or woman down. Turn to Performance Intelligence and arm yourself with the equipment necessary to reverse the trend. It could mean the difference between a high percentage of wins and just winning sometimes. Infecting your team with the five attributes of Performance Intelligence will give your group a common vocabulary for successful thinking. The proof is in the pudding. What do you have to lose?

5

Focus

"Doc, it's Clay. I got the speaking gig with Disney. No rabbit trails allowed on this one! Can you help me focus so I can do a great job?"

Clay Dyer is a professional angler. His motto for life is "If I can, you can." He was born with no lower limbs, no left arm, and a partial right arm. However, these limitations do not dampen his determination, drive, and dreams.

Clay started fishing at age 5 and began tournament fishing at age 15. He chooses to focus on the resources he has rather than on what he does not have. Whether fishing in tournaments or in practice, Clay tucks his rod under his chin to cast. He uses his mouth to change the hook or take off the fish. He ties the knots with his tongue.

When Clay is in front of an audience giving a keynote speech, there are bowls of cherries at each table. He challenges audience members to tie a cherry stem in a knot using only their mouths before he ties a new lure on the end of his line. Clay wins the challenge every time.

Highly competitive, Clay has not allowed his physical disabilities to be an obstacle, earning the respect of his fellow anglers on the pro circuit. A professional angler since 1995, he has fished in more than 200 bass tournaments and placed first in approximately 20 state bass tournaments.

Understanding focus is as simple as this question: When looking at a window, do you look at the glass pane or look through the window? Some will look at the pane, and some will look through it. There is no right or wrong answer. The exercise demonstrates that fundamentally, everyone knows how to focus. The challenge lies in learning where to focus.

Where to Focus

I've heard a lot of golfers talk about how they need help focusing on their game. I only have to watch them play for a little while to diagnose their issues. They drive the golf cart right up to the ball and look at the water, the sand trap, and the rough and consequently spend their time focusing on what not to do rather than on what to do.

"I've got water over there. I don't want to hit it there."

"There's a sand trap right in front of the green. I don't want to go there."

It is all a matter of aiming your focus in the right direction. Some people say, "Don't forget," and others say, "Help me remember." Some say, "I can't do this," and others say, "I am going to do this."

Top performers in any arena realize this subtle distinction. That is part of their ability to refocus after a mistake. It allows them to avoid making one mistake after another. If a sales call didn't turn out the way a top performer wanted, why dwell on that and have it negatively affect the next call and subsequent calls?

Shake off the residue of a mistake and learn how to apply its lesson. This is the pure application of Performance Intelligence. A top salesperson undoubtedly will be committed to a winning game plan. Because of that, the salesperson understands that sales is a numbers game. You win some, and you lose some. However, if someone makes 10 sales calls and is told "no" eight times, it also means that he or she heard "yes" two times.

Performance Intelligence allows a salesperson to understand these dynamics, how they fit into the big picture, and how to refocus. When you have confidence in your skills, it is easier to refocus, and refocusing requires self-discipline to make it happen. The focus shifts away from the mistake and to the correction.

Another characteristic of people who consistently perform at the top of their game is that they focus on the resources they have instead of the resources they lack. Talk to anyone in an organization of any size and you will hear about tight budgets and resources that have been taken away. The conversation focuses on what they no longer have. As in the case of Clay Dyer in the story that began this chapter, focusing on the resources you have sets you up to perform your best when it matters the most.

Playing to Win

Great athletes focus on playing to win rather than playing not to lose. You may remember that Olympic moment when many Americans watched Michelle Kwan skate in pursuit of an elusive gold medal. The pressure was too much. You could see how tight she was on every jump.

I would say that she was playing not to lose. This state is characterized by tentative, protective measures; the athlete essentially is trying to avoid messing up.

What was the difference between Michelle's long program and Sasha Cohen's program earlier that evening? With no expectations of winning the gold medal, Sasha simply went out to perform her best in the Olympic moment. She was focused on skating, not on the outcome. She was in the moment, doing what she loved to do. She was playing to win.

The difference between playing not to lose and playing to win is your focus. Playing to win is all about having a plan and implementing it. You focus on your plan. It motivates you, and you move forward. You let the win take care of itself.

Playing not to lose, in contrast, is not motivating. You are defensive, tentative, and cautious. There is a lack of excitement. You just play it safe. In fact, you really aren't even playing.

There is a great piece of dialogue in the movie *Chariots of Fire*. After losing a race, the character Abrahams says, "I don't run to take beatings. I run to win. If I can't win, I won't run." His girlfriend then states the obvious: "If you don't run, you can't win."

You have to PLAY in order to WIN. It doesn't matter how much you think about the points on the scoreboard in basketball. If you don't make good passes, communicate, shoot the ball successfully, and have intensity on defense, you aren't playing.

Think in terms of sales. When you are playing not to lose, you don't ask for the business. You are afraid of getting a "no," and so you don't give the client an opportunity to say "no." In that instance you protect the "yes." You play it safe. You continue to do the same things you have done in the past and hope nothing better comes along for your client.

Playing to win in sales has nothing to do with winning or losing the business. It has to do with looking at your clients' needs and finding ways to meet them. Let the win take care of itself. Going for the "no" can sound counter-intuitive, but it will keep you in the game. Allowing for the "no" is playing to win. Protecting the "yes" is playing not to lose.

The same thing is true for customer service. When you play not to lose, you hope the customer doesn't get angry at you. Playing to win is focused on responses that create exceptional customer service.

Singular Focus

To focus, your mind and your body must be in the same place. If your mind is 10 minutes ahead or 15 minutes behind you, you are not focused on what you're doing. Focusing on the present is a challenge in a society rife with multitasking.

When I work with someone who is having a difficult time keeping his mind in the same place he is, I have him use his watch as a cue. I ask him to tap his wristwatch as a reminder to keep his mind and body in sync. Many business executives could benefit from this exercise when they are at home. A busy executive can spend time with her children and not fully be present. Her mind is still at the office, wondering about sales quotas, meetings, and reports. This is not uncommon with our modern-day 24-hour availability.

Is she really there, or is she distracted and unable to focus on her children while sitting there for 30 minutes? Speaking from experience, I can tell you that children know the difference. They know when you're in the room, and they can tell when you're there only in a physical sense. A touch of her watch can remind an executive to focus on where she is physically.

Another technique to overcome the problem of tasks competing for your attention is to have a dedicated work space in your home. The space can be any size. Any time the job overtakes your thoughts, stop what you are doing and go there. Spend as much time there as you need to address the distraction. Once you are through, leave that space and return your focus to your home activities. This practice will help you focus and allow you to set boundaries if you find that your mind and your body are not in the same place. For other people, I suggest turning a light switch on and off when their minds and bodies are not in sync. You quickly learn how much time you spend focused and how much time you spend unfocused. This also gives you a chance to learn that you can be intentional about where you focus.

Of course, this flies in the face of our multitasking culture. Too many people who multitask believe they can handle an unlimited number of tasks with no dilution in their performance level on any of those tasks. After all, if you can do one thing well, why not take on six or seven things? The reality of that thinking is this: Whenever someone adds a second, third, or even fourth task, it results in diluted effectiveness on each additional task undertaken. This may seem logical to most people, but I have run into many a multitasker who does not believe that this is the case.

The need to multitask at times is understandable. However, I maintain that people who want to do their best when it counts the most should consider avoiding multitasking too often. When we show up and need to perform at our best, it requires focus. Too many of us rely on our minds to multitask, and we wear that approach like a badge of honor. If we always multitask, it creates a habit of divided focus. Diluted focus negatively affects a person's Performance Intelligence.

What is difficult to grasp about this line of thought is that we create a habit when we multitask. For example, I coached an executive who was in the process of relocating for his job. The timing of the move prevented his family from joining him immediately. Consequently, he was able to work 14 to 16 hours per day. He easily managed the huge initial workload because he had a 14- to 16-hour workday. Normally, he would have had a shorter workday because he would go home to be with his family. In our coaching, I asked him what would change when his family joined him in two weeks. Would he still work

14 to 16 hours per day? He answered, "Yes, my family is totally behind the move and will support me." I asked, "What does that look like? Are you still working during dinner?" He said, "Yes, if a call comes in, I will take it. I can review reports." I explained that he was moving from 100 percent focused to adding another area of focus: multitasking. Eating dinner with the family while working is multitasking.

He thought he would have the same results with this multitasking mindset. His thinking was not setting him up to succeed. I coached him to think about scheduling differently in preparation for rejoining his family because that exaggerated window of available time was an exception to the norm. Our coaching was geared toward a retooled winning game plan that would allow him to maintain the proper focus both at work and at home to achieve his desired results.

One of the most common illusions people have about focus is to think that they can be focused 100 percent of the time. A great example of this can be found in golf. One of the reasons players have a preshot routine is that it is virtually impossible to focus from the tee shot on the first hole all the way through walking off the green at the last hole. That is a marathon, and not a lot of people are trained to do that. Having a specific preshot routine trains players to understand when to start thinking about the shot and when to stop thinking about the shot.

Transfer that approach to the multitasking world, where the time to start and the time to stop blur your focus. Many activities simply bleed into each other with no clear pause. That is the primary reason a challenging conversation in the workplace, such as addressing an employee's perennial lack of attention to detail, is difficult. The problem with those conversations arises because we fail to focus and begin dwelling on issues on the periphery of the conversation.

Those conversations require a specific focus. If you start thinking about the conversation and what might happen four days before the conversation takes place, the dialogue is only going to become more difficult. Determine how long it will take you to prepare for the conversation. Once you schedule the conversation, always schedule sufficient prep time just before it.

A lesson for successful business leaders is that they need to value focus. Recognize that it takes time to gain focus. For example, consider adjusting your calendar to include preparatory time before meetings. Taking a proactive step such as that allows leaders to walk into a meeting with focus. After all, if leaders aren't focused on their meetings, how can they expect their teams to be focused? How can the information transmitted in a meeting be communicated accurately throughout the organization? Leaders have to focus on leading. It's not something that happens just by walking into the room.

Will there be distractions and interruptions that challenge your ability to focus? Of course, but what you do after a distraction is what separates champions from contenders.

If someone is performing his best when it counts and a distraction comes along, he refocuses on the purpose of the action and his plans to accomplish it.

Everyone has encountered people who are real champions when everything is going well. Then a diversion arises, and they become so distracted that they have difficulty refocusing. Distractions occur constantly in the business world.

The good news is that you can train your focus. When I work with clients who express nervousness about public speaking, I ask them to describe the condition. They invariably talk about having shaky hands. My advice is to squeeze a pen or grasp the podium while giving the presentation. That's focus. When your hands are occupied, they are tight and can't betray you by shaking. You no longer focus on your hands. You focus on your presentation.

Focus Past Your Mistakes

The Mind of a Champion facilitated a winning game plan workshop for a group of recruiters. We asked the participants to identify their thoughts about networking and prospecting for new clients. We asked them to look at their business plans and identify the thoughts that kept them from achieving their sales goals. After the workshop, we discussed our surprise that none of the participants had approached the Mind of a Champion team as a resource. I would have expected a group of recruiters to be prospecting at all times. Those recruiters missed an opportunity to tap into our network as a resource to help them prospect for potential candidates. We communicated our findings to the manager of the group, who asked that we bring up that oversight during our upcoming coaching conference call with the recruiter group.

The topic of our call was focus. We discussed the importance of focusing past mistakes. We pointed out the mistake. We coached them to focus past the mistake to the correction. The correction consisted of asking us about our network to see if we had any referrals as potential prospects for their candidate pool.

Because we focused past the mistake to the correction, we were able to coach the team members to improve their performance. Too often, coaching focuses on the mistake: Here is what you did wrong. Why did you do this? Will you do it again? Focusing on the mistake makes it more likely that the mistake will occur again. Focusing past the mistake to the correction increases the likelihood that the correction will happen the next time. You are coaching this correctly when the mistake is a sentence and you have a conversation about the correction. Too often we find the reverse. Leaders have a conversation about the mistake and the correction is only a sentence.

Clay the angler knew how to focus. As I coached him on his speaking gig with Disney, we discovered that when he focused on the audience, he could follow some rabbit trails in his presentation. We refocused on his message and watching his slides so that he could deliver his "Living the Dream" program with confidence. Focus provides half the foundation for a winning game plan. The other half comes from confidence. In Chapter 6 we will focus on confidence.

BUSINESS LEADER HUDDLE

Because I am a reformed multitasker, this chapter speaks to me. Focus is the first attribute of Performance Intelligence. Do you think that is by design? Without focus, Dr. Julie doesn't think we will get very far. Today's leader has to be all things to all people. To us, focus means being able to focus on five things at once. The reality is that we have gotten pretty good at it. We keep so many balls in the air that we have a hard time remembering when, or if, we ever did just one thing.

How does this message of focus compete with our sense of greatness at multitasking? There is no other way unless we choose to let a ball drop, right? Well, Dr. Julie is not saying that you shouldn't multitask. She is saying that when you multitask, you need to recognize that there is some decrease in focus for each new task you are doing simultaneously. This decreased focus affects performance.

"Good enough" may be enough for some of your tasks. But if you must perform when it counts, "good enough" may fall short.

This was the revelation for me. As a die-hard multitasker, I never realized that my performance was being affected. As she presented this concept to me, I quietly disagreed. I thought I was the exception. But her message resonated with me as I began to recognize my thinking about my diminished performance while multitasking. She was right. I now have a new focus routine that allows me to perform my best when it matters the most and recognize when I choose differently.

Performance Intelligence Challenge: Go one hour with a singular focus. Once you are successful with one hour, build to one day. The challenge will be to stop answering your e-mail when the phone rings and pay attention to the caller. Focus on each task individually throughout the day. In addition to your performance improving, you might find yourself being more efficient; this is the opposite of what you might think is true.

6

Confidence

"So, Alex, where is your tee shot going?"

"I think it might head down the middle, and then it probably will fade; I hope it lands down there by the bush."

"You have no idea where that ball is going, do you, Alex?"

"Absolutely not."

This was my first time on the golf course with Alex. He told me he was in a crisis of confidence with his driver. That led to my first question. His answer revealed his level of confidence in his shot: Think, might, probably, *and* hope *are not the most confident words to describe a tee*

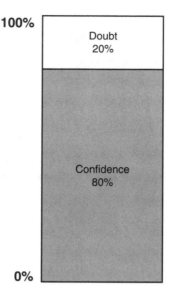

Figure 6.1 Confidence and Doubt

shot. With no confidence in his driver, Alex couldn't even settle on a target.

Confidence is an interesting topic. People often say they are 80 percent confident about something. If that is the case, I would argue that they are not so much 80 percent confident as 20 percent doubtful (see Figure 6.1). To be truly successful on a consistent basis, I believe you have to be 100 percent confident. You can have that confidence level if it's based on your predictable skill rather than an on unpredictable outcome filled with variables that are out of your control. For example, it is difficult to be 100 percent confident about getting a job because other people are involved in the process. However, you can be 100 percent confident in your ability to articulate, make eye contact, have a firm handshake, and do what it takes to put you in the best position to get the job.

Mistakes and Confidence

As was described earlier in this book, people make two common mistakes regarding confidence: being confident in the outcome rather than in the process of creating the outcome and having all-or-nothing confidence.

If you are 80 percent confident, the 20 percent doubt changes your skill. You may hesitate. If you are 40 percent doubtful, you will tell people in some form or fashion that they do not want to do business with you. The real problem with doubt occurs at the end of the experience: It precludes you from learning from that experience. Because the doubt has changed the execution of your skill, you do not know what to tweak because you have no idea where the doubt manifested itself. Maybe it was in the words you used. Maybe it was your body language. Maybe it was the way you presented the information. You don't know because you did not go in 100 percent confident in your skills. That keeps you from knowing which skills to train.

I coached an organization that put together a plan with a five-year goal. We were in year 1 of the goal, and the numbers were not on target. If the team had been confident only in the outcome of hitting the numbers, being off target in the first year would have created distractions, a lack of commitment, and fear. I coached the organization to be confident in the process rather than the outcome. They had the right people in place, along with the right leadership. It was the right goal at the right time. Staying committed to the process would lead to the desired outcome in five years.

How can I teach this so confidently? Think of Olympic swimmers. In the middle of the race, they touch the wall. The split time shows how they are doing compared with the world record and Olympic record times. It is possible for a swimmer to be off target at the first and second split times yet still achieve a new world or Olympic record. If the swimmer is completely focused on the outcome and his or her confidence rests in that outcome rather than in the process of getting there, knowing the split time will be a significant distraction.

The same thing is true in business. Your confidence has to be in the process of creating the desired outcome rather than just the outcome. Such confidence can remain high even if you are off pace halfway through. People tend to make several mistakes in this area. What if you've never done something before? Remember, confidence cannot be achieved in terms of an outcome; it lies in the ability to create an outcome. People say things such as "I will land this sale," "This audience will like me," or "They will benefit greatly from my message."

If you are a business leader, you cannot be 100 percent confident that your team will follow you. Too many variables are involved. What you can be confident in is your leadership ability. That confidence manifests itself as passion, commitment, decision making, vision, and team building. This is what inspires people to follow.

I believe it is a great idea to think about outcomes in terms of what you want, that is, having a goal and understanding what it looks like, sounds like, and feels like to accomplish that goal. That is a great motivator to train your skill. But if you're focused solely on the outcome the entire time, that will be a distraction, even during the event. The outcome as a goal is a great dream for motivational purposes, but once you get on the field, confidence must be based on the execution of skills. The outcome is not part of the picture. The outcome will take care of itself. Remember, if you do not get the outcome or result you desire, you can do something about that. You can identify the thoughts behind the actions that gave you the result you did not desire. Recognizing those thoughts, refocusing them, and creating new routines will move you a long way toward the success you desire.

As an example, I was coaching a client about a job interview. He was making a transition and wanted to be prepared to answer all the questions the way he thought the company wanted them answered. I stopped him and told him to play his game: focus on his strengths, what he does well, and his skills. I wanted him to understand that a job interview is for both parties: the candidate and the company. That means that an applicant needs to present who he is and allow the company to present who it is; then both parties can decide if the fit is good.

If he trained to answer questions the way the company wanted them answered, he would have to be prepared to spend the rest of his career at that company being the person it thought it hired instead of being himself. Confidence is a huge part of presenting oneself. As it turned out, he went into the interview full of confidence because he was focused on playing his game. It ended up being a great fit, but even if it hadn't, he would have been better off knowing that even if he didn't get the job. If your only interest is getting hired, you can train for that, but if you want the best outcome, you have to be invested in the process of achieving that outcome.

The second mistake people tend to make regarding confidence is having all-or-nothing confidence; that is an error because confidence is not that kind of quality. For example, those who play golf have had the unpleasant experience of walking off the green after a four-putt. It is fair to say that the golfer's confidence is shaky at best. She might even make a comment along the lines of "I can't putt today." That is an overgeneralization. Putting is made up of many discrete steps: reading the green, putting the proper pace on the ball, and rolling the ball on the golfer's line, among them. Are you doing any of that correctly today? Apply 100 percent confidence that you can roll the ball on the line. Then, when you miss the putt, you can learn from it. You pushed it or pulled it or you rolled it exactly on the line, and you need to pay more attention when you are reading the green.

If you believe you are either a confident leader or a non-confident leader, you are missing an opportunity to train some of your leadership skills. Leadership, like putting, is made up of a number of skills. Taking the perspective that you either have confidence or lack confidence misses the mark. For example, you could have rock-solid confidence in your knowledge, consistency, perseverance, and ability to focus but lack full confidence in your ability to manage your priorities effectively. With all-or-nothing confidence, you could overlook an area of skill you need to train or fail to acknowledge all those leadership skills in which you have great confidence. Lack of confidence in one area does not necessarily ruin the whole thing.

If a team meeting didn't go well, the temptation could be to say, "I am not a good leader." What are you truly talking about? Was your preparation lacking? Was your vision unclear? Was your passion in communicating the vision mediocre? If your evaluation of the team meeting is along these lines, you should be able to identify what you did well and what you need to change. That is, you can train that skill and increase your confidence so that you perform better the next time.

Confidence has a direct correlation to business development. I coached an organization that was focused on sharpening its business development abilities. The company understood that business development has a relational component, and the company representatives were teaching and training their people in relational skills.

In coaching them, the questions I asked were, "Do you have confidence in the skills necessary for business development?" and "What are those skills?" The company identified 10 skills that were part of the formula for success in past business development. In looking at those skills, the company learned that confidence had to be examined for each skill. It was not sufficient to say that any single person did or did not have confidence. Each skill had to be evaluated individually. Some partners were 100 percent confident in 9 of the 10 skills. The lack of confidence in the one skill of asking for the business led them to believe that they had no confidence in the entire process of developing business. It is possible that they never worked on a transition sentence to go from a casual conversation to a direct business conversation. If you break down all the skills and come to the conclusion that anyone can practice coming up with one transition sentence to increase confidence, that sentence can be the difference between landing the business and missing an opportunity.

With this new recognition of their thinking, the partners in the firm practiced developing any skill in which they were lacking confidence to increase their confidence in that skill. That led to an overall increase of confidence in business development. They got it. Confidence is not an all-or-nothing proposition.

The lesson in that example is that you must identify all the skills and traits required to have a successful outcome. At that point, you can define where you are and where you want to go next. Put another way, you can determine where you lack confidence and where you need to gain the confidence to perform within your skills to advance the goal you are seeking to accomplish.

As you list the skills involved, consider these two questions to move you toward success:

- How confident are you that a particular skill makes a difference in the desired outcome?

- What is your confidence in your ability to execute the skill?

If you are less than 100 percent confident in your ability to execute a skill, create a plan to train that skill. If you are still unsure that executing a particular skill makes a difference in getting to the desired outcome, you must make a decision. Indecision leads to procrastination and poor execution. As Yoda says, "Do or do not. There is no try." Determine whether executing a certain skill matters; if it does matter, do it.

Understanding Confidence

One of my favorite sayings about confidence came to me courtesy of one of the professional anglers with whom I work: "Confidence is the best lure in your tackle box."

That is worth considering for a moment. It speaks to us on several levels. It tells us that confidence should be part of our everyday equipment. It should be a natural part of our lives.

When I ask people "What does confidence *mean*?" they have a hard time coming up with a definition. However, when I follow that question by asking, "What does confidence look like?" they quickly begin to give me a list of things. They know it when they see it.

Confident people have their heads up and their shoulders back. They are walking with purpose. Simply put, they know their stuff. Confident people are comfortable in their own skin. Genuinely confident people are magnetic. It's true that we have a better idea of what confidence looks like than what it actually is.

The next question I usually ask people about confidence is, "When do you need it?" People respond with a variety of answers, ranging from "I need it when giving a presentation" to "I need it when attending a networking event." The real answer is that we *always* need to have confidence.

What I coach people to understand is the connection between confidence and a desired outcome. I often ask, "Do you have to be confident to have a desired out-come, or does a desired outcome make you confident?" This line of questioning causes a client to ponder her own confidence. Typically, the result is an understanding that if someone wants a desired outcome, that person must have confidence first. Once they understand this principle, my clients decide to train confidence in everything they do.

This applies to a golf workshop I was conducting. We were on the putting green, and I was explaining to the golfers how to train their confidence methodically. We talked about being confident in the process rather than the outcome. We talked about the skills involved in sinking a putt. Each golfer lined up three balls, and I asked them to focus on rolling the ball on their line. I wanted them to be 100 percent confident they could roll the ball on the line. After rolling her ball on the line she picked, one golfer drained a nice 20-footer. Remarkably, she then said, "Oh, that was lucky." Is it really lucky to do something intentionally and then achieve the results you intended?

Seizing the coaching moment, I said, "Every thought you have makes you more confident or more doubtful. Do you think 'That was lucky' makes you more confident?" I continued by pointing out there was no luck involved. She chose a line, she focused on rolling her ball on the line, and the ball went in. She had a plan. She was confident. She executed. Where's the luck? Your overall experience on the putting green isn't the determining factor for future success. What you think about your experience is the determining factor.

It is the same in the business world. I am working with a law firm on business development. They specifically want to have new attorneys begin business development in their first year. It is easy for those attorneys to get the monkey on their back that says, "None of my contacts are decision makers in regard to the choice of a law firm." The same attorneys will set up lunches. They will ask for the business, and when they get the business, too often they will say, "That was a fluke."

Just as with the "lucky" putt in the earlier example, was it a fluke? Or do you have the skills? Did you craft a winning game plan? Did you confidently execute that plan? Getting the business doesn't necessarily mean your confidence in business development will increase. However, the way you assess your business development skills will either increase your confidence or increase your doubt.

Often, I am asked to draw the line between confidence and arrogance. I consider the two distant cousins. Confidence is an internal belief. The way you demonstrate your confidence publicly can be characterized by others as arrogance.

Barry Sanders and Deion Sanders played football at approximately the same time. Each was very confident. However, each chose to display his confidence differently. One often was perceived as cocky because of his public presentation. The other was perceived as confident because his display was quiet. Internally, both believed they had talent. Confidence is internal. Arrogance is an external display of that confidence. Therein lies the difference.

You want your confidence to peak when it's game time, whether in the athletic world or in the corporate realm. If you have two seconds left in a basketball game and the team is huddled around the coach during a time-out, you want to tell your coach and teammates, "Let me take the shot." Many coaches know they shouldn't automatically default to the high-percentage shooter. They might be better served by choosing the player who confidently says that he wants the ball. It is possible that the others have some percentage of doubt, and as we now know, doubt changes skill. Which one would you pick?

Training Confidence

I recall being on the phone with my cellular service provider. The customer service representative took care of my needs. In fact, the way she communicated led me to believe she was confident in her skills. As we were about to end the call, I noticed a marked difference. It sounded as if she had begun to read from a scripted closing. I sensed a change in her confidence. She spoke more softly. She seemed unsure of what she was communicating to the point of being afraid.

I wondered if anyone had taken the time to explain the value of these simple but scripted closing statements. If I were coaching the organization, I would ensure that everyone understood the goal of exceptional customer service from the perspective of the organization's strategic goals. Without those goals in mind, the employees may think this part of the call is a waste of the customer's time. That thinking could result in failure to communicate confidently, thus altering the customer's experience. Coaching should not focus on the outcome: the response of the customer. Instead, it should focus on the organization's customer service process: applying the strengths and skills that allow the representatives to create an exceptional customer experience.

In my case, the customer service representative could have had extensive training in delivering the three closing sentences. However, if no one coached her thinking, her lack of confidence in those sentences would result in a poor customer experience. Confidence is an attribute that can be overlaid on any business skill.

My experiences in youth gymnastics lead me to believe that it is possible to train confidence. You do not have the luxury of being "sort of" confident when taking a skill from the floor to the balance beam. If you "sort of" perform, significant physical consequences can occur.

How do you train confidence? I coach my clients to begin by recognizing their successes on a daily basis. As a culture, we're great at recognizing failure. When you drive home at the end of a workday, what do you dwell on? Do you dwell on the things you have not accomplished, the things left undone on your to-do list? Too often, we do not spend thinking time on the tasks we completed. They are history. However, I coach people to stop and recognize the things they did, the actions they took that created the outcomes they checked off the to-do list. The checked items are their successes. Recognizing the actions necessary to create their daily successes is a key part of training their confidence for the next day and beyond.

Every time you recognize a success, you give yourself a reason to be confident. Likewise, each time you recognize failure, you give yourself a reason to doubt. Think about changing your approach. When you have a failure or make a mistake, transform it into a correction in your mind. If I am a gymnast standing on the balance beam and say to myself, "Don't fall," what am I thinking about? Obviously, falling. Correcting that thought, I would say, "Shoulders up." The mistake is focusing on what not to do. What-to-do thinking is focused on the correction.

As a business leader, you may recall a time when you led a disappointing team meeting. What was the mistake? Were you unfocused? What would be the correction? Maybe you could take 10 minutes before the meeting to organize your thoughts. You then could walk more confidently into the meeting with both thoughts and actions allowing you to achieve the desired result. When you focus on the mistake, it methodically trains your doubt. Refocusing your thoughts on the correction does the opposite: It increases your confidence because you have recognized that you have the leadership skills to lead a successful team meeting. Turning the mistake into a correction gives you confidence in employing your skills the next time.

Although we must keep our shortcomings in perspective, society challenges that. We exaggerate poor performance, preferring to wallow in it and expecting it to teach us a lesson. From a young age, you are either training your confidence or training your doubt. If your child is a 10-year-old soccer player and all you talk about is what she did wrong on the field, you are not training her confidence. However, if you ask about all the great plays she made on the field, you will end up having conversations that teach corrections and train confidence. Understand this: Dwelling on poor performance increases doubt so much that the next time we have an opportunity to perform, we approach it with more doubt than confidence. This yields an undesirable outcome.

Choose thoughts that make you more confident. Thoughts about your success will train your confidence. Recognizing success on the basis of where you are today will increase your ability to recognize success on a daily basis. We will come to understand a champion's definition of success and failure in Chapter 7.

BUSINESS LEADER HUDDLE

Confidence is king! This slogan often is used to refer to cash. I argue that without confidence there is no cash. Obviously, this is not 100 percent true, but it comes pretty close. You have to believe in what you do (on all levels) to succeed.

As it relates to confidence, the situation we find most business leaders in over time is that they become invested in the outcome. That's easy to do. With every promotion, the responsibilities increase. The stakes are high. You determine the goals, set expectations, and execute against those milestones. You must deliver or else. No wonder you are invested in the outcome. Your job depends on it.

How do we perform as Dr. Julie suggests by focusing our confidence on the process that creates the outcome and letting the win take care of itself? When we focus our confidence on the outcome, which often is made up of variables we do not control, we take our eye off the ball. We are less focused on the skills we need to create the outcome we desire.

Performance Intelligence Challenge: Return your focus to the process of creating the outcome. Your unique strengths and skills are the focus of your confidence. Determine the things in which you are

100 percent confident and those in which you are not. Train your skills to be 100 percent confident. This training is within your control. Executing on this will increase your confidence, and that will have a direct impact on the desired outcome. Let the win take care of itself.

7

The Real Bell Curve

"Doc, it's Bob. I've spent the past half hour trying to remember three things that were a success at practice. How long is this exercise supposed to take? I am having a hard time coming up with anything."

Bob is a collegiate tennis player. His practices are two hours long. He was in a slump when we began working together. I gave him a homework assignment: He was supposed to find (or recognize) his successes every day at practice. I said to him, "Did the ball ever go over the net?" He told me it did. I asked him to tell me about it. He told me about a topspin forehand to the deuce court, a line-drive backhand, and an average serve. I helped him realize that they were successes. Because they are part of his "everyday" game, he did not recognize them as successes. He discounted them while exaggerating his failures.

Within 24 hours of that conversation, he was out of his slump. He was able to go to practice the next day looking for success in the actions that took his game from average to excellent as opposed to seeing success only in the actions that fit his personal definition of perfection.

Remember, every thought you have makes you more confident or more doubtful. To train your confidence, you have to recognize your success on a daily basis. To recognize success, you must accurately define what success means to you: your personal definition of success. All too often, people exaggerate their failures and minimize their successes. In fact, our culture trains us to do just that. From a very young age, we were given back homework assignments with big red circles around what we have done wrong. Our teachers marked our papers with minus 10 or minus 7, highlighting the places where we failed.

My coaching of Performance Intelligence teaches people how to recognize their personal success, their personal failure, and what it means to be average. When you implement the tools in this chapter, you will have more success on a daily basis because success breeds success.

Are You Okay Being Average?

We need to recognize success, and to recognize it, we must be able to define it. Each person has a personal evaluation scale. Because it is personal, you should use only your own

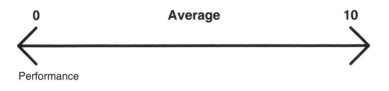

Figure 7.1 Personal Performance Evaluation

scale for evaluation. I don't recommend evaluating yourself according to someone else's scale. Your performance must be based on your personal strengths, skills, and talents. Rating yourself by using someone else's scale would not produce results consistent with your personal definition of success. Here is an opportunity to learn more. Figure 7.1 shows a personal performance evaluation.

The scale is easy to process. On the far left is 0. This side of the scale is reserved for actions in which you messed up so badly, you hope no one was watching. On the far right of the scale is 10. That represents the superwin. It is the exception to your everyday actions. It could be the ESPN highlight. The middle of the scale represents your average: the place in your performance where you are on a consistent basis today. A weekend golfer cannot use Tiger Woods's drive as average. Average is where you consistently perform today. That is why it is so important to understand that this is a personal performance evaluation.

I encourage the clients I coach not to be distracted by the word *average*. Let's be honest. Few people want to be average. The great news about realizing that you are average is that you also understand that you have more game in you. Performance Intelligence resonates with people because it is based on the premise that you have a higher level to your game. Embrace your average. It means that you know where you stand. Now let's unlock your inner coach, which can help take you to the next level.

As we come to understand the scale, I like to ask my clients how bad a performance has to be before they consider it a failure. If average is where a person is consistently today, how far below average would a failure or mistake be? Most people would say that anywhere below average is failure. I agree with that evaluation.

The next question, though, is more telling because it reveals intentional thinking. How good does a performance have to be for you to consider it a success? Many people will say it has to be a 10. As was mentioned earlier, a 10 is reserved for exceptional performances. These performances happen infrequently. Therefore, if you define success only as a 10, by default, everything else becomes a failure (see Figure 7.2).

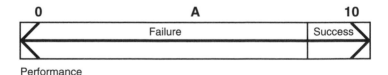

Figure 7.2 Inaccurate Definition of Success

In a professional setting, using an inaccurate evaluation in which only 10 is a success will lead to frustration, lack of motivation, and burnout. Sadly, it also affects your entire life, not only your work. For instance, many of us operate from a to-do list. Let's say a person tends to accomplish on average about 50 percent of what's on the list on a daily basis. If on a particular day someone accomplishes 7 of 10 items on the list, that would be above average. Imagine that person's drive home that particular day. What is he thinking about? Is he focused on the seven he finished, or is he dwelling on the three he didn't get to that day? That's the issue in a nutshell. Are we recognizing our successes (the seven), or are we looking at those things not completed and labeling them as failures? As you read this, you may be laughing about the fact that you often think more about the three things left undone. Many of the people I coach are in the same boat. They may dwell on the three because anything less than a 10 on the personal evaluation scale may be seen as a failure.

There is a real consequence to inaccurate evaluation. On the drive home you have company: a car full of monkeys on your back. They are telling you everything you have not accomplished. That thinking leads to feelings of stress and anxiety; in general, you feel like a loser. When you finally arrive home, you're feeling like a loser. As you open the door, you feel like a loser. Most important, your family greets you exactly the way you feel—as a loser.

Figure 7.3 Accurate Evaluation of Success and Failure

Consider this alternative: If average is where you are consistently today and everything below average is failure, everything average and above has to be called success. With this refocus in our thinking, how might the drive home be different? We drive home from work reviewing success: the 7 items we accomplished on our 10-task list. We feel like a winner. We open the door like a winner, and the family greets us exactly the way we feel—as a winner (see Figure 7.3).

Quick tip: Drive home looking at success. Drive back to work refocusing from mistake to correction. When you refocus on the way to work, it gives you enough time to plan and prepare for change rather than wallowing in failure. Remember that average is where you are consistently today; below that is failure you can correct and then move on.

Deep down, we all have a fear of being average, and that fear will keep us from accurately evaluating our performance. Very likely, you know a person like Bob. He says, "It makes sense that average to excellent is success. But this won't work for me. I know that I am harder on myself than anyone else. That's what makes me perform better." My response to this is, "Are you truly performing better?" The answer is no. His thoughts lead to frustration, lack of creativity, lack of motivation, and burnout. It's not because Bob isn't trying. It's because regardless of what he does, it's not seen as being good enough.

Your New Average

If average is where you consistently are today, this says that there is room for improvement. As you improve your skill, the performance you previously referred to as an 8 will be a 7 six months from now, meaning that you have more game in you. As you define your new average, you take your game to the next level. Your average is improving. This is good news. Your performance is average and will always be average, but it's your average. This scale does not encourage mediocrity. A performance someone pegs as a 10 today may be a 7 a year from now because that person is more talented and skilled. This requires the person to evaluate his or her individual performance accurately.

Success is a powerful motivator. When people see themselves as average and perform at a level of 7, they are excited about an above-average performance and eager to develop themselves and improve their skills. Figure 7.4 shows the average for someone we'll call Joe Smith.

Another illustration of this concept can bee seen on a golf course. I ask a golfer, "What is your average tee shot on hole number 1 on your home course?" He says, "Two hundred fifty yards to the left center of the fairway." Then

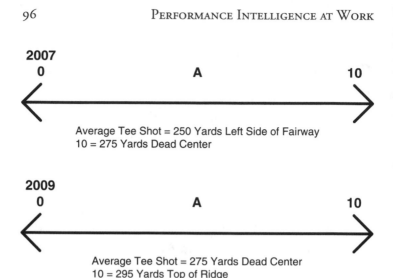

2007

0   A   10

Average Tee Shot = 250 Yards Left Side of Fairway
10 = 275 Yards Dead Center

2009

0   A   10

Average Tee Shot = 275 Yards Dead Center
10 = 295 Yards Top of Ridge

Figure 7.4 Joe Smith Is Average

I get agreement that anything better than 250 yards to the left center of the fairway is above average.

Next, I talk about how this player evaluates his shot on the weekend when he is playing with the guys. I know that he really wants to play well when he is with this group. When he is with the guys, he is looking for a 10, and anything less than a 10 is failure. Play out this scenario.

He is playing with the guys on the weekend. He hits his first tee shot 260 yards to the left center of the fairway. It is above average but not his best tee shot ever. Since this is an important game, the shot frustrates him because it isn't perfect. He is still left of center, which is where he is consistently—his average. He unintentionally evaluates it as a 4 on a scale of 1 to 10. That evaluation only sets him up for more frustration on the second tee box when he tries harder. As with many endeavors, it is difficult to hit a great tee shot when you are trying too hard. Although his tee shot on hole number 1 was truly above average, he inaccurately evaluated it as a failure. Because it increases your doubt, failure leads to more failure. Doubt negatively affects your skills.

Accurate evaluations are important because other words can replace *success* and *failure*. Every time we have a failure, we give ourselves a reason to doubt our ability. Every time we have a success, we give ourselves a reason to be confident in our ability.

The same approach can be used in the workplace. When a new employee arrives for the first day on the job, a number of tasks are introduced and must be organized. The new employee can do a few things and do them well while remaining organized. A year later, that employee has tripled the number of tasks she can handle and do well while staying organized. What a new employee thought could be handled in terms of responsibility has changed dramatically from what it was on the first day. With experience, her average has improved. A few years later, it may change yet again. An employee who develops additional skills and better handles more and more responsibilities raises her personal standard. What was once average in terms of organization and execution has changed because of the employee's ability to learn and grow—and take her game to a higher level.

A business leader is in essence the coach of a team, and that team will have regular team meetings. Some of those meetings will involve an average performance by the coach, and some of the boss's performances will be above average. It depends on the leader's focus and other contributing factors. When the leader conducts an average or above-average meeting, she must recognize that as a success and reinforce the skills that created the outcome. That level of self-discipline—recognizing success on a daily basis—is an acquired skill that will lead to more success in team meetings.

Beware of "Meets Expectations"

In the corporate world, the traditional model of performance evaluation is that the company wants you to, at best, fall in love with or, at minimum, be satisfied with "average." The dreaded "meets expectations" awaits you. The trap is often that the average the company is referring to is not your personal average; it is the company average. The company average is based on someone else's scale. It is based on the traditional bell curve. It does not take into account your personal performance relative to your consistent daily performance. I find that my clients do not want to be average compared with other people. This is understandable. We all want to excel.

For these reasons, it has been my experience that people don't like performance reviews. They don't like to conduct them, and they don't like to receive them. A lot of anxiety about participating in them can be found on both sides of the table. I coach organizations to rethink their brand of performance review. The performance scale must be on an individual basis rather than a general corporate level. It should reflect the fact that my average is my average and your average is your average. We need to move away from the corporate average model. I laud organizations that are moving in this direction.

I was inspired when I read *Built to Serve* (McGraw-Hill, 2007), in which Dan Sanders discusses setting a goal for the individual and measuring performance against that stated goal. This sets up fantastic performance reviews because everyone is evaluated on his or her personal performance. Your average is now a standard and a positive thing. It is where you are consistently today. Now your manager can coach you effectively on moving your game to the next level.

An individual average puts performance ratings in perspective. People want to know if they are meeting expectations because they truly want to improve their skills and take their performance to the next level. That is a true coaching environment.

The Four Quadrants

To summarize our horizontal graph again, average to excellent is considered success and below average is failure. That is the performance scale. Now add another line that bisects

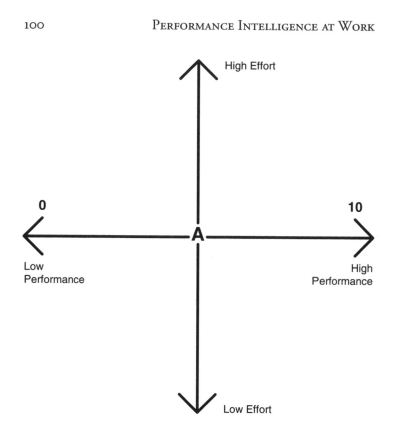

Figure 7.5 The Four Quadrants

the performance scale, creating four quadrants. We'll call that effort and look at how it factors into each quadrant of performance. Whether we have high or low effort, if the performance is average or above, it must be called a success (see Figure 7.5).

Let's visually walk through each quadrant. I use a megaphone as a symbol to describe someone in the high-effort, high-performance quadrant (see Figure 7.6). The

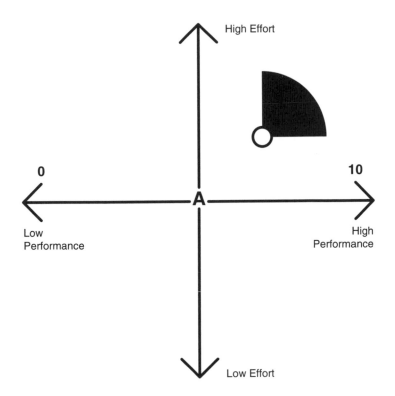

Figure 7.6 High Effort/High Performance

higher the effort and the better the performance, the more likely you are to view that as a success. For example, you work nine months to close a half-million-dollar sale. At the end of the day of the closing, you may tell your spouse, your neighbors, or your friends. In your own way, you recognize that success. However, on the day you land an average sale that took an average amount of time, are you still recognizing that as a success and reinforcing that success by sharing

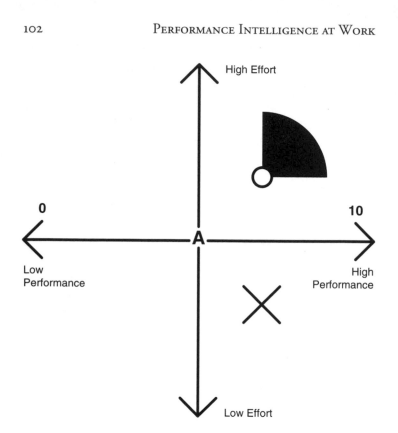

Figure 7.7 Low Effort/High Performance

it? Most people would not. The coaching moment here involves teaching you how to recognize that everything in this quadrant is success.

Now we move straight down the graph to the low-effort, high-performance quadrant (Figure 7.7); here the visual is an X. This is where someone says, "It doesn't matter." It was a good performance, but if it was easy, it doesn't count. For most of us, this quadrant represents at least 80 percent of the day. It is a matter of training ourselves to do these simple things and do them well. The tendency is to discount them because it's just what we do. We seldom think of these mundane tasks as successes. For example, one person's effort to be punctual may require high effort. For another person, the goal of timeliness requires low effort. The important fact in both instances is that timely arrival is a success regardless of the level of effort. Basketball players consider the layups they make as too easy to be counted as successes. However, if a player misses a layup, that's considered a failure, and so making one merits treatment as a success. If it is a failure when you don't do it, you must consider it a success when you do it.

The visual in the low-effort, low-performance quadrant is a sad face (see Figure 7.8). Let's be honest here. This quadrant is where we messed up. Don't spend too much time here. This is the point where we refocus from the Monkey on our back mindset to the Determined mindset. Use more effort or polish some skills to create a different outcome. We simply need to identify the problem and make a correction. A correction is what *to do*, and a mistake is what *not to do*. Identify it, address it, and move on.

My favorite quadrant really opens people's eyes. This is the high-effort, low-performance quadrant, and the visual here is a circle with a line through it (see Figure 7.9). People fall into this category when they say they cannot change. Unfortunately, it is not a matter of their inability to change.

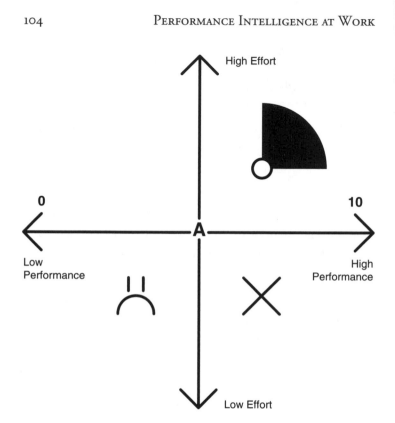

Figure 7.8 Low Effort/Low Performance

It is more a function of the fact that they inaccurately define what they are doing to begin with. You hear statements such as "I've tried really hard, but I didn't get the results, so I can't change." With further investigation, you might find that the performance wasn't below average. It just did not reach perfection.

The fitness world is full of examples of this. A new year rolls around, and one of the most common New Year's

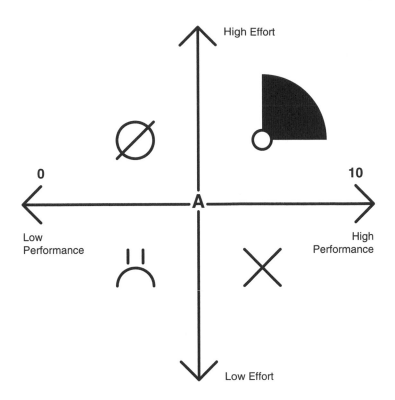

Figure 7.9 High Effort/Low Performance

resolutions is to get in shape. A person who makes this resolution decides in his mind to make it to the gym three days a week for 20 minutes each day. That is his 10. The same person's average is walking around the block once a month. January 2 arrives and the alarm is set, but when it goes off, he hits the snooze button and falls back asleep.

Normally, any human would evaluate that as a miserable failure. I coach people to think of it as a success.

At least the alarm was set correctly. On the scale, this person isn't below average because he at least thought about going to the gym. The alarm goes off the next day, and the person makes it to the gym for 15 minutes. Traditionally, we would evaluate that as a failure because the person didn't stay the full 20 minutes. I coach my clients to think differently. The reality is that he was there for 15 minutes. Actually, he is now way above his personal average. Instead of thinking in terms of failure, this person is having success and eventually reaches three workouts a week for 25 to 30 minutes. That is greater success, and when anyone has success, it makes that person feel good and motivates him or her to pursue more success.

One final point. I refuse to get hung up on the word *failure*. Many people are uncomfortable hearing that word. I used it freely in this chapter and do so when coaching people. Sometimes I use words such as *mistake* and *messed up* because we hate to hear the word *failure*, but the reality is that if you have messed up, you must be able to call it a failure. It doesn't mean that the person who made the mistake is a failure. The action or lack of action is the failure.

Our performances do not define us. Our actions create a failure just as our actions create a success. But actions at work and on the golf course are not who anyone is as a person. A failure is simply a mistake, and a mistake always has a correction. That's important because the correction allows people to learn and grow.

BUSINESS LEADER HUDDLE

I think this chapter is critical to understanding Performance Intelligence. Dr. Julie's position on success and failure is eye-opening for business leaders. Once you absorb what she is saying, you may respond the way I did. I remember thinking that the real bell curve makes so much sense.

It's all too easy to compare our performance with that of someone else. How ridiculous is this in light of Dr. Julie's perspective? Everyone possesses a unique set of skills and strengths. Each of us is at a different level of his or her Performance Intelligence. How we perform every day is our average. I was hired on the basis of my average, knowing that I can improve. I've got more game in me.

Everyone needs a personal definition of success. After fully embracing this, I now approach every professional pursuit with a different perspective. I want to answer the question, "What does success look like for this event?" Determining the success milestones allows me to know my target. It also keeps me vigilant so that I do not define success in terms of things over which I have no control. Success is based on my average. Success is based on my actions rather than on the outcome.

The classic example is the job candidate preparing for his final interview. How do you define success? "Getting the job," he says. Really? How can he define success in terms of something he does not control: the granting of an offer for employment? Instead, refocus your thoughts on things you do control: Present to your abilities, communicate your desire for the job, and have fun along the way.

Performance Intelligence Challenge: Take time this week to break down your leadership skills and define your average. Once you know your average, you can evaluate your successes accurately and correct your mistakes or failures. Knowing your average reveals that you have more game in you.

8

A Winning Game Plan

"Dr. Julie, I know how you can help. I want more focus in my workouts, and I need help with my thinking. I tend to psych myself out right before adding more weight."

Michael was a competitive bodybuilder who wanted to compete at the next level. I knew I could help him with his focus. Focus is directly related to having a winning game plan. However, I was a little surprised when we discovered that "psyching out on bumping weight" also is related to having a winning game plan. Without a winning game plan, Michael would second-guess his workout routines.

Get out your Tinkertoys. It is time to build a winning game plan, and Tinkertoys are a great visual. If you gave everyone in the room a set of Tinkertoys and time to build, each person would create a unique structure. People use resources differently, and each individual has a different idea about how his or her structure should look. Although there would be similarities resulting from sharing ideas and information, no two structures would be exactly the same. This will be true for you as you build your personal winning game plan.

Every great coach comes to the field in each season with a winning game plan. That plan gives the coach and the players direction. The plan can be tweaked throughout the season, depending on the circumstances, the health of the team, and the quality of the competition.

I will draw parallels to sports more in this chapter than in any other. The sports analogy creates a compelling model to motivate you to create your own winning game plan.

A Game Plan or a Winning Game Plan?

Do you wake up every day knowing what you need to do and having the motivation to do it? If you do not, you could be going through life with only a game plan instead of a winning game plan. Perhaps you have multiple game plans: one plan for your professional life and a different plan for your personal life. You may find yourself failing to achieve your goals in both areas. You procrastinate, disappoint others, or find yourself stressed out. Often, when game plans in different areas of life conflict, it is difficult to meet the expectations of both. Only after identifying the areas that compete and cause distraction can you synchronize multiple game plans to create a unified winning game plan.

I knew Michael's focus would improve once he created a winning game plan. He would have purpose in his workouts and the necessary motivation to stay on track. His confidence increased with the understanding that his workout would get him ready for the competition. His winning game plan would minimize distractions and create a system for tracking his workouts. This plan would capture his purpose. Michael knew what I was talking about. He had a game plan to add bulk and then taper off the weight to be ready for the competition. He needed a winning game plan incorporating his workout plan.

A plan like this can help with decision making, as my experience coaching a team of supervisors has revealed. During an individual coaching session, a supervisor named John explained his struggles with the decision to apply for a promotion involving relocation.

When talking to John, I realized that the promotion was only one of many decisions with which he was struggling. He was concerned about how relocation would interfere with his desire to settle in his hometown eventually. He weighed not taking the position against his ability to move up in the organization. He even considered exploring positions outside the organization. John was distracted and was losing confidence in his ability to make decisions. He did not have a winning game plan, and so he was trying to make decisions in isolation when he knew they would affect his choices in the future.

He did not have a plan that identified whether a promotion involving relocation would create a desired result for his professional and personal lives. Imagine John's ability to stay focused and confident in the decision-making process if he had a winning game plan. It would be a check-the-box decision instead of what seemed like a life-or-death choice. He could use his winning game plan as a tool to increase his confidence in his decision making and also to stay focused on his goals and desired outcomes.

On the basis of his background, I knew John could execute a plan he believed in. He was a highly successful athlete. He lived at the Olympic Training Center while growing up. He followed a plan designed by his coach outlining what skills to practice, when to hit the weights, what to eat, and when to sleep. John's experience in executing a winning game plan as an athlete provided the motivation to create a winning game plan that would serve him well in his professional pursuits.

The same is true for you. Do you wake up every day knowing what you need to do and having the motivation to do it? Do you approach decision making with confidence? The first step to building a winning game plan is to define your win.

Think about an NFL team that wants to win the Super Bowl. To get to the Super Bowl, the team must win playoff games. To make it to the playoffs, it has to win several games. To win those games, the players must make touch-downs by making first downs. To make first downs, the coach has to have a winning game plan. When he calls time out on the field and brings the team together, he isn't coaching the team on the score. He is getting the team focused on executing the winning game plan. Without a winning game plan, you can coach only on the results rather than the execution of the plan. With a winning game plan, you are able to coach on the skills it takes to execute your particular plan.

Businesspeople know how important this can be. A team leader who takes the end-of-quarter sales numbers into a coaching session with his team and talks solely about the results is missing a prime coaching opportunity. He would serve the team better by bringing the winning game plan to the coaching session and helping the team recognize the relationship between executing the winning game plan and the results. Connecting the dots to show how thoughts lead to specific actions that result in the execution of the winning game plan leads to the team's desired results. This is the business leader's real coaching opportunity with the team.

Defining Your Win

Your win is your personal definition of success. A common misunderstanding in the corporate world is that everyone has the same win. I do not believe this is true. People are motivated differently and aspire to achieve different results. I see this in every organization with which I work. Take a highly successful law firm. One attorney's win is making partner status, and another attorney's win is bringing in the most new clients. Still another attorney's win is working flextime.

In a sales organization, I see one distributor focused on meeting his goal and another distributor focused on exceeding her goal by 10 percent. In sports, one runner wants to win the marathon, another runner has a specific time goal, and still another has a stretch goal that is simply to cross the finish line.

An important part of this process is defining your win so that you can celebrate along the way regardless of the size of the victory. Celebrating along the way increases confidence in you and in those who are playing the game with you. What would it be like to go to a football game at which you sat quietly in the stands until the end of the game? If your team wins, you finally cheer. If your team loses, you remain silent. I can't imagine too many people getting excited about a game like that. Instead, we cheer for the incremental wins along the way. We cheer for touchdowns. We cheer for first downs. Depending on your team, you may cheer even for forward progress. You will have wins along the way toward your personal goals for success because your winning game plan is built on a foundation of your strengths.

Leveraging Your Strengths

As was explained earlier, every great coach has a winning game plan. Part of that plan is to prepare for the upcoming season. The coach starts with an assessment of the strengths of his players. He focuses on both the strengths of the individual and the strengths of the team as a whole. It has been my experience in business coaching that many organizations begin their planning sessions by focusing on what is not working and then write a list of necessary actions to make improvements.

My approach is aligned with the sports model used by great coaches. I recommend recognizing the strengths of your team and what is working before you take a look at what is not working or what you want to tweak. You may find that when you use my recommendation, the only thing that needs tweaking is your thinking. You may discover that you have the right people in place, the right process to meet your goal, and the right goal. The only thing you need to change is the coaching relative to execution; that means that you will train your team to recognize the thoughts that led to poor execution and coach its members to refocus on thoughts that will change their actions. The new actions will lead you right where you want your team to be: executing a winning game plan leveraged on their skills, talents, and resources.

We train this approach in the Mind of a Champion's winning game plan workshop. Our clients spend the first part of the workshop answering this question: What is working? The answer to this question helps us identify their strengths so that we can coach them to continue to be intentional in those areas. We find that our clients may neglect to do the things that have created success when they are distracted by undesired results.

Undesired results? We all have them, right? After building a foundation on what works, you continue to build your winning game plan by looking at what does not work. Take a look at the results you consider undesirable. If you agree that thoughts lead to actions that lead to results, doesn't it make sense that undesired results come from actions that start as thoughts? When you recognize your thinking and refocus your thoughts to align them with your strengths, you identify actions that lead to the results you seek. When you practice doing this consistently, you will execute your winning game plan absolutely and effectively. We refer to this process by using the acronym TAR/RAT (see Figure 8.1).

I was coaching a group of executives around the time of performance reviews. We were doing some coaching in the moment, and so I learned that several people on the leadership team were not completing performance reviews

Thoughts → Actions → Results

Results → Actions → Thoughts → New Thoughts → New Actions → New Results

Figure 8.1 TAR/RAT

for their team on time. This was not an isolated incident. History revealed many markers of delayed or missed performance reviews.

I asked the leaders what they were doing to address this issue. One suggested putting the reviews on her calendar. Another suggested color-coding the calendar. Still another suggested setting alarms on the calendar. I have a lot of suggestions about how to do things in a timely manner, but those leaders did not need coaching on actions. They needed coaching on thinking.

I asked them what they thought of performance reviews. The overwhelming perception was that no one liked them. They couldn't see any real value in them except as a report on which to base bonuses. We addressed that thinking as I coached them to refocus on the benefits of the performance review as well as thoughts regarding their strengths as leaders and the role they played in the professional and personal development of their team.

Once the leaders could think differently about performance reviews, they were able to change their actions and put the new actions into an improved winning game plan.

Making Tough Decisions

Executing a winning game plan includes making decisions. In facing a tough decision, you have to evaluate the following: your circumstances, your plan of action, and your strengths, talents, and resources. Can you see how your winning game plan serves as your resource to make tough decisions? Your winning game plan gives you permission to say no. It is an effective tool to use in situations that can easily distract us, taking us off track.

I remember watching Vijay Singh at the PGA Tour Championship several years ago. He found himself about 100 yards from the pin, but he was in the rough with a dozen trees between him and the green. I'm sure he had hit out of the trees many times in his professional golfing career. However, these circumstances were different. He really didn't have a shot between the trees or over the trees.

Anyone who knows golf understands that from 100 yards out, a professional golfer puts the ball on the green, usually near the pin. Vijay did the unthinkable. He turned away from the pin and knocked the ball into the middle of the fairway. With that one action he set himself up to succeed. It turned out to be an incredible story. From there he holed out. It seemed amazing when he knocked it into the cup from the better lie in the fairway, yet the lesson would be the same even if he had left it a few feet from the pin.

My interpretation is that the decision he made after realizing he didn't have a shot from the trees was part of his winning game plan, which had been determined long before the situation arose. The important thing to note is that before the tournament, I believe Vijay already had determined that good course management was an element of his winning game plan. Good course management included the possible action of turning away from the pin for a shot to better his chance of success. Because that decision already had been made, when he was faced with a low-percentage shot over trees, he effectively decided to enact that course of action without distraction. Using his winning game plan, he made a tough decision that gave him the opportunity for greater success.

A winning game plan is important for corporate athletes as well. Plenty of opportunities for tough decisions will present themselves. You must evaluate your circumstances while executing your winning game plan. Taking the right action may not be intuitive. Don't follow the textbook if the situation calls for something else.

Tough decisions are not made 100 percent in the moment. They follow your winning game plan and your evaluation of the situation. Do you speak up in a meeting even though it is not expected that you will have a compelling thought or question? Do you stay late to help a colleague with a project even though it doesn't affect you directly? In the face of a tough sell, do you oversell your services because you really want the business?

I can't answer these questions for you. The decisions are yours. However, I can tell you that a winning game plan will make these tough decisions easier. A winning game plan directs your tough decisions. Be intentional in your decision rather than simply defaulting to the typical textbook choice.

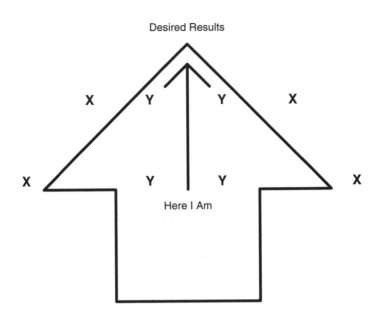

Figure 8.2 A Winning Game Plan

Your winning game plan points to your win, as shown in Figure 8.2. The closer you get to your win, the more intentional you must be in your decision making to realize that win. What may have started as an acceptable decision becomes a marginal decision as you progress toward your desired outcome.

In five years, you want to take a family trip to Europe. Your winning game plan includes putting money aside for the trip. In the first few months of executing this winning game plan, your daily trip to a coffee shop may be an acceptable decision. As you get closer to realizing the win, it is possible that the daily coffee run is affecting your ability to move toward your goal. With a winning game plan, every decision you make is an intentional decision. Without a winning game plan, every decision is merely a decision. Determine your win. Be intentional about the decisions necessary to achieve the win and execute your winning game plan.

Executing Your Winning Game Plan

To win in any game, you must play. Executing your winning game plan is playing. Executing that plan will allow you to stay intentional about keeping your strengths strong and having the confidence and self-discipline to develop your weaknesses. Just as in sports, you will continue to tweak your winning game plan. Pay attention to times when you are executing the elements of your plan and times when you are not. Examine the actions and follow up by recognizing the thinking behind those actions.

A winning athlete or a winning team plays to win. The athletes have a plan and work the plan. The coach, the fans, and the players reward them on the basis of the execution of the plan. Cheers, high-fives, and congratulations come not only for final results but for executing the plan that created those results.

I often challenge executives on their plans. I ask them about their confidence in their plan to produce the results they desire and whether they reward on the basis of the outcome of the plan or on the basis of the execution along the way. A perfect example of this came when I was coaching a sales organization. Before my coaching, the managers wanted the team members to have 45 new contracts by the end of a certain period. They would reward each team member for each new contract. After creating a winning game plan, they had the confidence to begin rewarding the team for making the calls that led to the new contracts. Having a winning game plan allows leaders to reward on the execution of the plan, thus encouraging their teams to continue to play to win until they break through the tape at full stride.

With a winning game plan you know where to focus. You have confidence in the skills it takes to execute that plan. Your winning game plan will encourage accountability, a key factor that is discussed in Chapter 9.

BUSINESS LEADER HUDDLE

Do you have a winning game plan? After reading this chapter, do you want one? As a business leader, think how much time you spend distracted by the things you focus on outside of what would be your winning game plan. Without that plan you have a hard time determining the opportunity cost for your professional time. The tyranny of the urgent can force itself on you. So much time is spent putting out fires, there is little time to focus one's actions on the tasks necessary to move one's goals forward.

An interesting point that Dr. Julie makes is that you cannot have inconsistent winning game plans. Although this book is dedicated to Performance Intelligence at work, the application to your personal life is obvious. As you think about creating a winning game plan for work and for your personal life, those plans must be consistent. Think about the CPA whose winning game plan includes being home with his family for dinner at 6 p.m. During tax season he cannot possibly be home before 8 p.m. If he does not tweak his two game plans into a winning game plan, he will be distracted at work each day as he chronically misses his departure time. As a result, he will set the wrong expectations at home.

Performance Intelligence Challenge: Decide today that you want a winning game plan. Pick one area of your professional responsibilities or duties. Determine the results you desire. From this point, you can establish the actions you can take that will lead to the results you desire. From those actions you can form the thoughts that will set you up to succeed. This is a winning game plan that will keep you intentional. Writing out the plan gives you the ability to focus beyond the hectic activity of your day. The performance that you generate will increase your confidence in your winning game plan.

9

Self-Discipline

"Doc, I am thinking about skipping practice tomorrow. Do you think that would be a problem?"

Heather was a collegiate swimmer. She had been swimming since she was 10 years old. She had self-discipline. Swimmers put in hours in the pool nearly every day; some days they swim twice a day. Heather was at a point in her career where she was questioning whether she should stay in the game. Was it time to retire? Without a commitment to play the game, self-discipline is a real challenge.

Self-discipline is the attribute of Performance Intelligence that causes many people to roll their eyes. The word itself may cause you to think that this will be your least favorite attribute. If that is the case, let's recognize that thinking.

Any time someone asks us about our goals, one of the first things we mention is that we need a bit more self-discipline to achieve those goals. That is the paradox of self-discipline. We know we need it, we desire it, but we don't really want to talk about it.

Desire to Improve

I have worked with a number of athletes in a variety of sports. Even after all my work with athletes, I remain amazed at the training and effort necessary to create a champion: football two-a-days in the August sun in Texas, early-morning gymnastics workouts with repetition of routines until the athlete's calluses peel and bleed. In addition to such grueling workouts, athletes have to adhere to other elements of their winning game plan: meals, curfew, and dozens of other details. Can a nonelite athlete tap into that kind of self-discipline?

Absolutely. The common denominator among great athletes is a desire to improve. They want to improve and then remain consistent. I have found that most people say they want to improve. On the basis of their actions (and therefore their thinking) I question whether they really do. Research indicates that 45 to 55 percent of Americans want to lose weight, yet only 15 to 20 percent say they work a plan to reach that goal. Do you just say you want to improve, or do you really have a desire to improve?

Training your Performance Intelligence will help you perform your best when it matters the most. Performance Intelligence training is for anyone, from a 10-year-old gymnast to an 80-year-old angler and from an executive assistant to a CEO. It is available for anyone but is not for everyone; that means you must have the desire to improve before you can perform your best when it matters the most.

I was coaching a manager on taking his team to the next level. He defined the next level as a promotion, and so he thought that everyone defined the next level in those terms. He knew that a majority of his team members were not interested in moving. The ability to relocate was a requirement for consideration on the promotion list. His misunderstanding of the next level affected his ability to coach his team. Remember, when I speak of the next level, I am talking about performing at a higher level: greater consistency, better accuracy. As a leader, you must define the next level before you can lead team members to the goal. A good friend of mine is a teacher. He is always looking for ways to be a better teacher, to take his game to a new level. He had a meeting scheduled with a student to help her with math. A family issue called her out of town, and so she went to the teacher to reschedule the meeting. He learned that she had an iPhone and offered to make a podcast of the math lesson that she could download for her trip. A good teacher connects with the students in the classroom. This teacher took it to the next level.

You can't make people want to be better. I have found that that must be an innate desire. Performance Intelligence helps unlock the coach within you to realize that desire and allow you to take your game to the next level. This teacher demonstrated it.

Accountability

As we have said, great athletes have a winning game plan that dictates what they need to do. The difference between their record of success and that of others is that they have self-discipline. They have confidence that taking those actions will create the desired results. Self-discipline complements the first two attributes in a simple manner: It is a matter of doing what you say you're going to do.

Self-discipline is all about being intentional. I see self-discipline as something different from willpower. In my mind, willpower is a fist pump. Take one for the team. Grind it out. Finish the race. Self-discipline is more of a handshake. You have said you want to change. Now you shake hands with a teammate, a coach, someone else, or yourself to establish accountability; this is what I call voluntary accountability.

When you choose voluntary accountability, you bring your mistakes to light and ask for coaching. You seek help to correct a mistake. When I was working with a group of supervisors in a call center, the supervisors complained that they would be blindsided by a call from an upset customer. They would have to take that information to the agent for a "coaching moment." The supervisor was not excited about this coaching. The agent knew the customer was upset but chose to pretend the situation would go away.

Voluntary accountability dramatically changes that scenario. At the core of voluntary accountability is a fundamental change in your thinking. Instead of the monkey on your back nagging you about the mistake, you choose to think about the experience differently. You want to understand your thinking, and you reach out to someone to coach you through recognizing your thinking.

Replay the agent scenario. Through voluntary accountability, that agent would go to the supervisor and say, "I just had a call that did not go well. This is what happened. Can you coach me so that I can be more effective next time?"

The supervisors agreed that voluntary accountability would make their job easier. They could be more effective in their management by using this style of coaching. Instead of the agent feeling that she would get in trouble by revealing the poor performance on the call—the equivalent of being sent to principal's office—the agent would approach it differently. She would go to her supervisor for coaching because she was tapping into her innate desire to improve. This shift in thinking caught the supervisors' attention during this workshop, and so I continued to explain how to introduce voluntary accountability into the call center. They would have to model the behavior.

You can imagine the feeling in the room. The supervisors were uncomfortable thinking about modeling voluntary accountability. I could read their minds from the looks on their faces. They may have been thinking, voluntary accountability sounds great. I really want my staff to operate that way. It will solve many headaches for me. But if I to have to implement it for myself, I am not so sure about this.

Telling them that introducing this wonderful self-discipline concept to their team would have to start with them brought a new level of thinking to the group. It meant they would have to go to their manager and say, "I messed up here. Can you coach me to improve?" Voluntary accountability cuts against everything we know and nearly everything we have learned and been taught since we were young. When my three-year-old does something wrong such as taking a toy from his sister, he does not come to me with voluntary accountability. He acts in the opposite manner by running and hiding. At our core, it is hard to own up to our mistakes. I want to encourage you to realize that adherence to self-discipline through voluntary accountability will take your game to the next level.

Leaders, take note. When a team member comes to you with voluntary accountability, you cannot overreact to the circumstances of the mistake, something that could be very natural for you. Get in the Determined mindset. Put on your coaching hat. Recognize the benefit of voluntary accountability. Refocus from the mistake to the correction. Coach this person so that she can have this routine of voluntary accountability—a new habit of the mind.

When a runner has trouble getting off the blocks, he goes to his coach for improvements. When a basketball player can make free throw after free throw in practice but continues to miss in games, she goes to her mental coach. Athletes recognize where they need coaching and then choose voluntary accountability to take their game to the next level. You can do that too.

I was at dinner with my husband and told him about my strong desire to be a better mom. We have a winning game plan that includes parenting, but I know I am not consistent in following the plan. I know when to use discipline with the children and how to work my schedule so that we can spend time together as a family, but sometimes it takes more effort than I feel like making. I said, "If a supernanny was sitting on our couch, I know I would be a better mom. That accountability would help me be more intentional. For example, I would stop what I am doing and look into the eyes of my children every time I am speaking to them."

Because hiring a supernanny is not in our plan, I asked my husband to let me be accountable to him. He would not have to ask me how things were going. Instead, I would talk to him about whether I was or was not following our winning game plan. With this handshake agreement, we committed to voluntary accountability.

A few days after this dinner conversation, I scheduled a coaching appointment on a Saturday morning. I often have Saturday morning appointments, but this was different. I had been out of town for a few days. I needed to be home with my children on this particular Saturday. After making that mistake in my scheduling, I went to my husband and said, "I messed up." I asked him to help me work through it and coach me so that I could perform better for our family the next time. That conversation allowed me to change the way I schedule appointments. If I had not chosen voluntary accountability in that situation, the conversation would have been very different. I would be heading out the door feeling some guilt. A simple question from my husband such as "Where are you going?" would have put me in a defensive posture, not a coachable mindset. Voluntary accountability not only was good for me as a parent, it also was good for my marriage.

I was leading a quick huddle coaching workshop to teach leaders how to be more effective coaches. One of the business owners in the group said, "I know how to do this. I know I can go back and be a great coach to my team. But in a couple of weeks I will end up back the way things were before." I said, "I hear you asking for voluntary accountability." When you have the desire to change, choosing voluntary accountability will keep you on track. I asked him to schedule time on his calendar in about 10 days for coaching. He would make the call. He would talk about the execution of his winning game plan. He would choose voluntary accountability.

Initially, there is nothing natural about voluntary accountability. When you initiate voluntary accountability, you may need to get into the Determined mindset. At first you will feel uncomfortable. That is okay. No one leads an organization from the comfort zone. The great news is that the more you do this, the more natural it will become.

Be Consistent

Besides the fact that self-discipline helps you take your game to the next level, it will help you be more consistent. Once, when I was coaching a team of real estate agents, one agent couldn't understand how she could have a great month and then dip so low the next month. She felt as if she were doing things the same way. The actions she took were, in her mind, consistent. However, they did not produce consistent results. When we created her winning game plan, she realized that her prospecting would diminish during her high-production months, leading to lower performance later. Not keeping her sales funnel full at the top rippled into the next month's performance. Being intentional about marketing regardless of sales became part of her winning game plan.

Consistency is defined as more than consistency in your actions. Performance Intelligence training takes into account consistency in your thinking as well. When you are winning, you think like a winner. When your performance drops, are you still thinking like a winner? One of my swimmers was in a slump. We were talking about her thinking during practice. She realized that when she was winning, she reviewed a highlight film in her mind during training. However, during her slumps, she spent her time in the pool wondering what was wrong. She wondered, Am I really a winner? This inconsistent thinking limited her performance consistency.

There is a way to create that highlight reel, but it requires self-discipline. When you are doing well, record your actions. Journal your strengths. From time to time, read about your success, remembering what it took to be a winner. This is more than a matter of thinking positively. It includes identifying the thoughts you had that led to actions that produced results that created success. Replaying those successes and the thoughts that got you there reinforces better habits in your thinking. Having the self-discipline to do this journaling activity during good times, when everything is going your way, is the key to consistency for the challenges ahead.

Another technique I recommend to athletes is to produce an actual video when they are playing well. This production can include some performance clips, but the focus is on the athlete's thinking. I ask athletes to create a recording of what they are thinking before, during, and after practices and competitions. The next time the athlete has a slip in performance, she can watch the highlight reel and remember what she did to think like a winner.

Take the lesson from the collegiate golfer on his way to turning pro. As part of his college team, he had a sense of belonging. That allowed him to draw on the collective team strength to think like a winner. When he was working his way onto the tour, he thought he had to prove himself. He was not yet one of the guys. He did not yet belong. The change in his thinking produced inconsistent results. His performance suffered. Taking it one step further, he looked at what the other players were doing and built them up until he found himself squarely in the Intimidated mindset.

I helped him create a winning game plan, allowing him to focus on the thoughts that set him up to succeed. That increased his confidence. It was self-discipline that made all the difference. For him, it was the glue that bound focus, confidence, and his winning game plan. For you, it can be the tie that binds these elements together for increased Performance Intelligence. Choose today to enter the realm of self-discipline. If you find yourself with low self-discipline, you have a high need for voluntary accountability. You will be in that determined mindset with voluntary accountability. But if you do it long enough, it will become natural.

BUSINESS LEADER HUDDLE

Self-discipline. On its face this is not a touchy-feely word. It means you have to do something. You actually have to execute. If this book resonates with you, you are probably naturally self-motivated and self-discipline as a concept may not be that challenging.

Dr. Julie turns self-discipline on its ear. In Performance Intelligence, self-discipline is in large part voluntary accountability. What is voluntary accountability? It means that you should approach each situation by thinking about how you can catch yourself as opposed to being caught. But we are not trained to expose our mistakes. We have to show that we know everything and are 100 percent perfect all the time.

As a business leader, think about the burden your staff lives with if the monkey on their backs is similar to the perfect standard described in the previous paragraph. Dr. Julie does not advocate mediocrity. She does encourage people to catch their mistakes and seek coaching. Are you approachable as a leader for this type of relationship with your staff? Can they come to you with their mistakes and ask for coaching?

A business leader once told me that he expected his staff to make decisions. For every 10 decisions they made, he didn't mind if they made five mistakes. In those five mistakes he found the coaching moment. Through that experience and his coaching, the staff members learned more than they would have if they had never made the decisions. Although he expected them to learn from their mistakes, he reflects the core of voluntary accountability. Decide today to create an environment of voluntary accountability for your team.

Performance Intelligence Challenge: To create an environment of voluntary accountability, you must model it. Choose self-discipline today and reach out to someone with whom you can be accountable. Discuss the area you want to improve. Share your winning game plan. Then set up times to talk about your execution of that winning game plan.

10

Competitiveness

"Doc, I was playing an amazing round of golf until I hit hole number 13. It was a nice par three that played to my 8-iron beautifully. I was just about to pull the club out of my bag when I noticed that another guy in our foursome had pulled out his 9-iron. He and I had been pretty competitive the entire round, so I pulled out my 9-iron and didn't even make it to the green. What was I thinking? I know better."

When John plays his game on the course or in business, he is a competitor. When he shifts from playing his game to focusing on beating a competitor, the outcome is rarely what he desires or what it could be. This call marked the first time John recognized that his poor execution was based on his thinking.

Make no mistake about it: Competitiveness is a good and healthy thing. Competitiveness is part of the Performance Intelligence equation because performing your best when it matters the most requires inner drive. That desire to win, whatever your win may be, keeps you in the game regardless of the particular outcomes along the way.

Many people have that internal drive, that competitive spirit. For a person to be successful, it must be focused in the right direction so that it leads to the desired outcomes. Competitiveness includes motivation to achieve, competitive outcomes, and a competitive playing field.

Motivation to Achieve

In Chapter 9 we talked about having the desire to improve your performance as an essential element in self-discipline. Competitiveness brings that desire into greater clarity. Some people have a strong competitive nature to achieve success. Others have a competitive nature to avoid failure.

Having had this conversation with a number of athletes and business professionals, I find it interesting when people try to convince me that the desire to avoid failure is motivating and is good for their performance. I believe it can be motivating, but I do not agree it improves performance. Thoughts to avoid failure are not necessarily thoughts that lead to actions that produce results you desire. You may perform well a number of times, but consistency will be elusive.

If your desire is to avoid failure, we are talking about fear, which limits your performance. The fear of missing a free throw creates tension in the shooter's body, making it difficult to get off a good shot. You can see how fear affects performance in sports. I lead a boot camp for golfers a couple of times a year. At the camp, we mix Performance Intelligence classroom lectures with on-the-course activities designed to improve an athlete's mental game and thus his handicap. One of the on-the-course experiential learning activities is for the golfers to play nine holes without a golf ball. Can you imagine this?

I learned the true coaching value of this activity during a one-on-one session on the course with a client. It knew it is a great learning tool for visualization, and I realized it is an even more valuable teaching tool in regard to fear.

Think about how this plays out. The player goes through his complete preshot routine and then hits an imaginary ball. He actually has his club in his hand and is swinging as if there were a ball on the tee. The player visualizes where the ball lands. He then walks to that spot for the next shot with the imaginary ball. The process continues through all nine holes. After about three holes, the players get a little more comfortable with the activity and settle into their playing. By the end of the round, they have discovered their game without fear.

When you remove the possibility of hitting it in the water on the right and no longer are preoccupied with avoiding the sand on the left, you can focus on playing your game. I watch each golfer who tries this slowly settle into the Natural mindset. As you can imagine, every golfer at that boot camp ends up saying to me that he played his best round of golf at boot camp. No doubt about it. They did not play outside of themselves by imagining amazing once-in-a-lifetime shots. Each simply played his game without fear. There is great freedom in picking your target, executing your shot, and moving on toward the successes that result from your winning game plan.

I have applied this philosophy to corporate coaching. When the desire to avoid failure is stronger than the desire to achieve success, you play not to lose rather than playing to win. You can achieve a certain level of success—even be very successful—but I bet you have more game in you.

A business leader gave me a call to learn about my coaching, and I was curious to learn why he wanted coaching. From everything I had read about this person, he was successful. When we met, he told me about his motivation to achieve. That motivation came from fear, and it was wearing him out. Instead of being excited about his vision and moving forward with passion, he thought about what would happen if he was not successful. How would he pay his mortgage? How would his lifestyle change? Those fears kept him awake at night and pushed him to succeed during the day.

I want to remind you that he was very successful. He had implemented this fear model for motivation for a long time. He worked hard in college because he didn't want to be thrown out of school. He built his business out of similar fear. But he desired a change. That motivation to achieve left him stressed and near burnout.

We refocused his competitiveness toward success and learned that he had more game in him. Better yet, he could enjoy the game along the way. Do you enjoy your game? Are you motivated by your vision of success or by your fear of failure? Research supports what I have experienced in coaching relationships: You can be successful with both motives to achieve. But my personal coaching relationships lead me to believe that performing your best does not come from a desire to avoid failure. It comes from a strong competitive attitude toward success.

Competitive Outcomes

The way you explain your successes and failures provides insight into your competitive nature. Do you take credit for your wins or attribute them to luck? Do you take full credit for your failures or attribute them to external sources? It may surprise you to learn the mindset of champions.

Champions take full credit for wins. They believe that success comes from factors under their control such as talent and effort. For example, an applicant for a supervisory position goes into an interview with a plan and a purpose. She comes out with the job. She attributes the success to her skills and preparation. Skills reinforced, confidence gained.

A person without strong competitiveness may attribute success in the interview to weak competition. The company defaulted to him because no one else was more qualified. Less successful competitors attribute wins to factors out of their control, such as luck.

I coached a young banker on his goal to increase his business development. He believed that since he was a young professional, his network would not be sufficient to bring good contacts or new business to the bank. His peers weren't in decision-making positions within their organizations. They did not control decisions on the banking relationship. Even though he thought this, he set up a lunch for the sole purpose of business development. At the end of the lunch, he had the business. He said, "Oh, that was a fluke." That did nothing to reinforce his skills. He experienced no gain in confidence. In his mind it was just luck. That interpretation left him believing he was still not good at business development. When you believe you are not good at something, it hinders pursuing success with passion and commitment.

To perform your best when it matters the most, you must take full credit for your victories without minimizing your part in the successful outcome. This will increase your confidence and your motivation to continue playing the game.

After a loss, highly competitive athletes may attribute failure to external factors. Maybe they had a poor strategy or an opponent played in a lights-out way. This keeps a competitive athlete ready for the next game. When an athlete attributes the loss *only* to poor skills, confidence diminishes and hope for a better outcome the next time is low.

I'm not saying that competitive athletes don't recognize their mistakes and make corrections. What I am saying is this: When they look at the competitive outcome, they attribute the loss to factors outside their control, knowing they've done their best. It does not shake their confidence in their skills and abilities.

I was coaching a college swimmer just before the NCAA championship. He was talking about how awful his season had been. He said the only reason he was in such good standing at that point in the season was that somehow he "managed to pull off" a win in a meet. He described in great detail the reasons for his poor performance. Asked to describe the win, he found himself at a complete loss about why he had performed well.

The mindset of champions is the exact opposite. When you win, you know you are responsible. When you lose, there has to be a reason, and that reason is not your skill or talent. I am not saying you cannot have a poor performance. Of course you can, and that performance can be related to mistakes you made or other external factors. What I am saying is that one poor performance does not call into question your skill or talent. Examine your thinking as well as the external factors to allow yourself to focus on the correction. Elite athletes have trained new habits of their thinking to do just that, and so can you.

I know that some people are uncomfortable when we apply this champion's interpretation to the business world. People are all in favor of taking credit for success, but can a leader really allow her team members to attribute poor performance to circumstances outside of their control? Isn't that just making excuses? You can follow the model of athletic champions if you are coaching correctly.

When you coach your team, you have to help them recognize success. Review Chapter 7 to remember how to recognize success as being on a continuum from average to excellent. You will recognize the actions that created the success, not just the outcomes.

Then you can help coach your team members to refocus after mistakes. A lousy quarter is a mistake. If a team member wants to attribute that to an issue at home rather than his communication skills, I would not have a problem allowing him to do so. It is quite possible that the home issue was a distraction. We have learned that it affects one's performance when one is not focused. When I coach, the mistake is only one sentence. Refocusing on the correction is the paragraph that leads to the overall conversation. The team member attributing the mistake to outside influences still believes in her skill and can be back in the game the next week. If the low performance is happening on a consistent basis, your real issue is not with the excuses. It lies in your coaching. Are you having a conversation about the mistakes and allotting only a sentence to the correction? Putting it a different way, do you still believe in that team member? Have you coached him on the hard skills involved in his job? Have you coached him on focus, confidence, and a winning game plan? Does this person have the desire to change?

In business and in sports, champions take full credit for victory and distance themselves from failure after identifying what needs to be addressed.

A Competitive Playing Field

When your competitiveness is focused for success, you turn your attention away from beating the competition and toward taking your game to the next level. Rather than focus on beating the competition, focus on improving skills and working toward your personal best. Accomplish that and let the win take care of itself.

I was coaching a supervisor in the technology industry who was extremely competitive and wanted to be number one on the team scorecard. I asked her to shift her focus from the scorecard to her game. Where was she performing at 100 percent of her ability? Where was she falling short of that 100 percent goal? When her focus shifted to this area, she was able to be intentional about taking steps to improve the skills in which she was not performing 100 percent to her capabilities. Over time, this positioned her to be number one on the scorecard.

I have seen this happen repeatedly in sports. When an athlete focuses on the competition, he distracts himself. It sets up the playing-not-to-lose mindset. When an athlete is focused on playing her game, it is about playing. Research on peak performance supports this. When a person is in the zone or experiencing a peak performance, he is in the moment. He is doing what he is trained to do. He certainly isn't focused on the outcome or on beating the competition.

When Michael Jordan was cut from the team as a young player, he made a commitment. Was the commitment to focus on winning the game the next time he played? No. The commitment was to realize his full potential as a player. That competitive focus on taking his personal game to the next level served him well.

I talked about Jim Dawson and Zebco in the introduction to this book. Jim definitely knew what the competition was up to, but he kept his team members focused on performing their best at all times in all circumstances. A competitive spirit is valuable. A desire to win is a great attribute. However, that competitiveness must be focused in the right direction: taking your game to the next level.

Creating Win-Win

Everyone puts a face on competition. If you can't identify the competition easily, my advice is to pick someone closer to your sphere of influence. The best way for an organization to grow is to fill itself with people who challenge one another in a healthy, productive way to reach the next level.

The first sign that this is happening within an organization occurs when someone's success motivates others to strive toward previously unexplored heights. For years, observers believed the running of a sub-four-minute mile was physically unattainable. Roger Bannister believed he could accomplish that goal. After years of training, he succeeded. It might surprise you that within eight weeks John Landy was able to achieve the same milestone. Further illustrating this point, 16 other runners shattered the four-minute mile during the next three years. Bannister's success as the first did not defeat his competitors. It spurred them on to greater success.

This reflects a more sound approach than the typical model in many organizations, in which someone else's success defeats everyone else because they didn't win. The same circumstances occur when people play not to lose rather than playing to win. They become protective and decide not to share their best practices. Have you noticed that some of the most successful companies happily give away their best ideas? I'm not talking about proprietary information. Rather, these are corporate philosophies that allow people to contribute to the organization's success.

A number of companies shy away from this. They fear that telling someone else their philosophy will result in another organization using that information and doing better. Whether it's individually or organizationally, the best way to address that fear is to get that thinking out on the table and talk about it. When someone or some company is playing to win, competitiveness is focused on playing, and the win takes care of itself.

A healthy organization creates an environment where people can say, "I've been doing this. Now you take it and grow it." When we consider competitiveness, many organizations have internal competitions that provide fun and entertainment on a weekly level; that is another way of having a game within a game. Someone closes a big sale, and the company decides to celebrate it in a unique way that encourages healthy competition.

Are you playing with your teammates or against them? Before you answer, think about this: If your teammate wins, does that mean you lose? If you win, does that mean everyone else loses? Win-lose is a zero sum game, a game of scarcity. Someone always wins, and someone always loses. Win-win offers a better way. This allows each person's individual success to spur on the successes of others. Win-win is a game of abundance.

The win-lose mindset is pervasive, entering every area of our lives. We use it in terms of our competition and our team and even at home. Expanding your concept of competiveness will allow you to develop win-win relationships. You can celebrate the victories of others, while allowing them to motivate you to raise your game to the next level.

BUSINESS LEADER HUDDLE

Throughout law school and as a practicing attorney, I was trained to win. If you did not win, you lost. I never wanted to lose. I wanted to win. I wanted to be a winner.

By being focused only on winning, I lost sight of just playing the game. The motivation for my preparation was to perform in order not to lose. I was intensely focused on my competition and slipped right into the Intimidated mindset. If I could only work harder, I would prevail. I came to the competitive table with the perspective of win-lose. It became a grind.

The trap I fell into is exactly what Dr. Julie warns about in this chapter. This is a distraction, and decreased focus affects performance. The concept of win-win changes this dramatically. As I transitioned to the business world, I quickly learned that focusing on the win-win was a more successful (and enjoyable) way to manage my teams.

Performance Intelligence Challenge: Create an environment that promotes the win-win concept. When everyone on the team can celebrate and is motivated by the success of another team member, you will know you are on the right track. Additionally, as your team members begin to focus on the competition, refocus their thoughts. Remind them of the facts: your team's key differentiators, strengths, skills, and past successes. This reinforces new habits of the mind and sets the team up for success. You focus on playing your game, and winning takes care of itself.

Performance Training Center

"Doc, I believe everything you just said. I know that changing my thinking will improve my performance. But I have no idea how to make that happen right now."

I was in the first year of my career. I had just spoken to a group of competitive cyclists when Kerry came up after the program. His piercing comments made sense. How do you know if you are training your mental game? How do you know if you have recognized and refocused and are creating routines?

What descriptions do you apply to the world's finest athletes? "A powerful server." "An arm like a rocket."

"Good hands." "Championship outlook." "A winning attitude." Frequently you might describe those athletes as "mentally tough." When we talk about all-star athletes, we are just as likely to mention their mindset as their physical skills.

Take a moment to think about how much of your game is mental. Regardless of your chosen pursuit, whether you are a doctor, lawyer, or lumberjack, pause and reflect on the mental part of your game. I often ask groups, "What percentage of your game is mental?" Depending on the sport or profession, the answers fall within a range of 50 percent to 90 percent. There is a mental component to learning a skill and executing that skill successfully. The follow-up question I ask is, "How much of your time do you spend training your mental game?" More often than not, they answer, "I don't know."

This chapter is the result of that conversation with Kerry. Here I have outlined strategies for training your mental game. When we work with an organization, we explain up front that a keynote presentation is designed to make an impact. An impact is great. Usually when I hear a good speaker, I feel the impact. However, a couple of hours or days later, I yearn for the true change spurred by the speaker's message.

As I describe an impact session such as a keynote presentation or a workshop, I am quick to inform the organization that real change comes from the deliberate reinforcement of the message. At the Mind of a Champion, we call that spaced repetition: delivery of the message in a way that consistently reinforces the themes to create new habits of the mind that lead to productive actions.

Think back to when you were in school. Once you were presented with a concept, the teacher often gave you homework to reinforce that concept. This chapter will give you the homework needed for the spaced repetition of the message that will train Performance Intelligence and develop the Mind of a Champion. Understanding a few fundamentals will help you attain the best results.

Visualization

Visualization is a common technique that sports psychologists teach. Many people have heard of the value of visualization but believe they cannot do it. When someone tells me he cannot visualize, I ask how often he practices visualization. This question makes the point that it is a skill that can be trained. If you can "remember when," you can visualize.

I honed my ability to coach visualization when I was working with a 10-year-old gymnast. We started simply. I asked her to describe her house. I asked her about the colors in her room. I asked her what stuffed animals were on her bed. Next I asked her if she had ever had other stuffed animals on her bed. Her answer of "yes" led me to ask her to close her eyes and move the animals around on the bed. She easily did that.

Next I asked her if she had ever watched *Cinderella*. I asked about the colors and sounds in the movie. We played a little "remember when" game. Again, she did this easily. Soon we were ready to move the visualization exercise to the gym.

That practice helped her understand the power of the visualization skill, allowing her to gain control over the movies in her mind. She used the skill in the gym and on the way home. At practice, she would visualize an upcoming skill or routine while waiting in a line. On the way home, she would visualize corrections. If she was working on a specific improvement, she could zoom in or visualize it in slow motion. That allowed her to perform better.

You can use visualization to improve your skills and increase your confidence. As you prepare for upcoming performance reviews, visualize yourself challenging your employee to step up her game. Hear your firm voice, see your reassuring face, and feel your heartbeat increase as the employee becomes defensive. Continue to play it out in your mind as you see yourself refocusing the conversation and communicating to your employee that you really believe in her.

The following two strategies build on your visualization skills.

Decisive Decision

To quote the renowned sports psychologist Bob Rotella, "The best decision is a decisive one." When you find yourself struggling to make a decisive decision, simply make the decision in your mind only and then spend a few days acting as if it were true. This is an extension of the visualization exercise.

Michael Brothers is a hairstylist whose business acumen is as impressive as his ability to provide customers with the perfect style. His calendar is booked a year in advance. He has been selected to carry top-of-the-line products. He has trained more than one apprentice to build a successful business.

Several years ago he was having trouble deciding whether he should stay at the current salon or make the move and open his own place. I coached him to make a decision and play it out for the week. He would make a firm decision in his mind and then go about the week as if it were true. If the decision created more stress and anxiety, he would reconsider it. If the decision gave him new motivation and a sense of peace, he was ready to move forward. At the end of the week he was able to make the move to open his salon.

Michael was able to implement the same strategy a few years later when deciding whether to stay at his current location or open a larger salon. He made a firm decision in his mind. He continued his business throughout the week as if the decision were final.

Whether you are making a decision to stay in your current job as opposed to starting your own business, a decisive decision must be made. Indecision leads to doubt. Doubt changes your skill. Changed skill affects performance. Make a firm decision in your mind. Use your visualization skills to play it out mentally. Then make the real decision with 100 percent commitment. Having done this, you can stand firm in the confidence that you made the right decision.

Experience and Expectations

Throughout this book, I have talked about how thoughts lead to actions and actions lead to results. Let's focus on improving the factors that influence your thinking. Your thoughts are influenced by your experiences and your expectations.

In regard to performance, it really doesn't matter what you experience. It matters what you think about that experience. I find that I can help many people take their game to the next level by having them think differently about their experiences.

For example, you had a two-hour practice. You did many things correctly. However, on the way home, you focused on the three things you did wrong. You went away from practice more doubtful rather than more confident.

Golfers are great at this. A golfer goes into the clubhouse after having his best round of golf, and someone asks about his game. He says, "Best round ever, but I missed this three-foot putt on the seventh hole." He then spends the next 10 minutes describing his mistake rather than reliving his best round of golf.

What you think about your experience directly influences your expectations. You had a difficult conversation with a business partner. The result was what you wanted, but there were some tough times in the conversation. Perhaps all you have focused on since the conversation was the difficult moments. The experience should have left you with confidence that you can have a difficult conversation that leads to a win-win outcome. However, because of your thinking about the conversation, you continue to doubt your ability in this area.

The way you interpret an event sets up your future expectations. In the broadest sense, you expect success or failure. "I will probably run late" is a simple example of expecting failure. I challenge you to recognize where your thoughts set you up for failure and where they set you up for success. The exercise described below will teach you how to interpret your experiences to set up expectations of success.

Journal

Journaling is a great way to know if you are training your mental game. It is an exercise in self-discipline. I encourage you to journal for 28 days to create a strong habit and then pick it up again from time to time when you need help refocusing. You will see the benefits of journaling within a week of beginning the exercise.

I am a fan of journaling for three reasons:

1. It holds you accountable. At the end of the day, you know if you did your homework.

2. It increases your focus so that as you write, you pay attention to training specific areas of your thinking.

3. It lengthens your attention span.

To receive the maximum benefit of journaling, I believe you should follow a specific formula, and I use the acronym WIN as a reminder. Go figure!

The *W* in WIN stands for *warmup*. If you are going to journal your thoughts, you need to take 30 seconds and write down every thought in your head from buying milk on the way home to the big presentation you have scheduled in two days. That gives you a half minute to warm up your brain, and that will help you focus on the next two important sections of journaling.

Target one specific area for improvement over the next two sections. If you are a golfer, you may choose tee shots, long irons, short irons, chipping, or putting. Choose just one area, though. As a business leader, you can focus on decision making, influence, team meetings, or business development.

The *I* in WIN stands for looking at the *ideal*. It gives you a chance to recognize your success. What did you do well today? What were the actions that created the desired outcomes? This is where you focus on your skills, your talents, and the utilization of your resources. Take the time to write down the things you did well that day. Remember that success is defined as average to excellent (see Chapter 7).

It is important to recognize your success with a period at the end of the sentence. What I mean by that is that when you look at what you did well, do not qualify why something is a success or discount the success. When you say, "I was very organized today, and I am usually not," you are undermining your success. You almost get a check mark in the confidence side of the scale, but you take it away with the last comment. "I was very organized today." Period. Let your success stand alone.

One mistake people typically make in journaling is to exaggerate their failures and minimize their successes. For example, salespeople may say, "I made three prospecting calls today, but I'm unsure if it will turn up any business because last time it didn't work." You discount your success for one reason or another. This exercise involves writing about successes only. You will have an opportunity to refocus your thinking about your mistakes in the next section.

The *N* stands for *new experience*. This is a time specifically established for you to correct your mistakes. A new experience starts with identifying the mistake. It can be a mental mistake or a physical mistake. Either way, you correct it by saying what you would do differently if you could do it all over again.

The new experience is where you play out your correction. You take the information, make the correction, and see yourself applying that correction as you visualize the new experience. For example, perhaps you were walking up to the lectern for a presentation in front of a large group of peers and tripped over a computer cord. Most of us continue to replay that awful event in our heads over and over and over again. We even go so far as to think about what the audience was thinking when it occurred. Leave that unproductive thought habit behind. Focus on the correction. It's easy: Just look where you are going. The new experience allows you to see it in your head. Visualize your new experience. You are announced as the speaker, you see the cord, you smoothly step around it, and you turn to the crowd and say, "Good morning." It is a valuable use of your time when you see yourself doing it correctly.

You went through the journaling process correctly if you spent more time describing and explaining the new experience than you did discussing the mistake. Too many people spend 15 minutes talking about a mistake they made, and when they replay the new experience, they do it in 15 seconds.

When I talk about journaling, I don't necessarily mean writing a story. Not everyone is a writer. You can journal in story form. You can journal in bullet list form. What I look for is whether you have visualized your success. You can journal vocally. Try it while driving home from work. Talk out loud. The process is not as effective if you just say it in your head. It will work if you follow the WIN process and do it aloud.

One other helpful tip is always keep white space for miscellaneous thoughts when you are writing down your successes and your corrections. As much as we try not to think about something, once it's in our minds, it distracts us. Write it down in the white space and release that thought.

Journaling is a way to know that you are training your thinking. It is an exercise in self-discipline. When you embrace the new experience and are creating a correction and playing it out, you must speak in a clear, confident voice that demonstrates that you have the skills to do it. Whenever you hear people using phrases such as "I might" and "I should," they have not made a decision. That indecision on a correction leads to poor results.

Finally, don't take on too much to journal. I tell clients to take one area to journal. You cannot do it about your entire day in one setting or it will take hours. Journal for 10 to 15 minutes either vocally or in written form. Journaling provides an opportunity for you to focus on specific desired results.

Journaling and Performance Intelligence

Focus: Most people have more control over their thoughts when they are writing or speaking as opposed to just thinking. The WIN journaling method will help you focus on recognizing your success and refocus on corrections to create new routines.

Confidence: The WIN journaling method will train your confidence methodically. Every time you look at your success, you give yourself a reason to be confident in your abilities. Every time you correct a mistake, it is like erasing a doubt check mark and putting in a confidence check mark. When you accurately apply the success-failure scale and look at success in the range from average to excellent, you will become more confident. More confidence leads to more success.

Winning game plan: Your winning game plan will give you direction in terms of where to focus for the WIN journaling. Recognize the results you are achieving in relation to your winning game plan. Refocus your thinking on the basis of the results that are not desired.

Self-discipline: Many of my athletes have a difficult time distinguishing between times when they are thinking about mental training and times when they actually are training their mental game. Keeping a journal will help you move from thinking about mental training to doing it.

Competitiveness: The WIN method of journaling keeps you focused on improving your game. As you journal, you will evaluate your average and look at success in terms of average and above-average experiences. Your journal is not about comparing yourself with others. It is about moving your game to the next level.

Performance Intelligence at Work

When we go to auctions, my husband wisely holds the bidding paddle because he knows I really want to be in the game. In fact, I don't care if I am bidding on a porcelain pitcher or an antique car. I just want to be in the game. Who cares if I win? I just want to play.

In my career, I have encountered only a small percentage of people who recognize that they want to improve their game and reach out to me for coaching. I know many more are sitting at the same desk day after day, going through the motions. They are just shy of giving up on themselves as they determine whether the risk is worth the reward. What I know to be true is that being in the game is better than being on the sidelines.

I am committed to getting people off the sidelines and into the game. Performance Intelligence unlocks the coaching voice that says: "You have more game in you."

Training Performance Intelligence equips you to realize the next level of your game: performing your best when it matters the most.

Employing the principles of Performance Intelligence will help you develop the Mind of a Champion. Enjoy the game.

BUSINESS LEADER HUDDLE

If you are like me, you enjoy going to events and hearing speakers. Those speakers are often informative and sometimes entertaining. In fact, after the message or presentation I find myself quite energized. Sometimes I am even motivated to go out and take on the day. However, within a couple of hours or within a day or so, I return to the premotivated status quo.

A great keynote definitely can make an impact. But if you want real change, you need to have reinforcement of the material: periodic reminders of the message. Dr. Julie prescribes spaced repetition as the reinforcement necessary to develop the Mind of a Champion. As part of this prescription, she encourages experiencing the content by doing the activities.

Performance Intelligence Challenge: Show your leadership by working on your Performance Intelligence. This chapter gives you tools to do that.

Go through the exercises provided in this chapter. The results will be helpful for your Performance Intelligence. Changes in your thinking will take your game to the next level. You are now equipped with personal examples that will encourage your team.

Specifically, as you begin to introduce your team to the principle of Performance Intelligence, you can use the exercises in this chapter. Sharing your experiences will be a good model for them. You are now prepared to coach them from your understanding of Performance Intelligence.

Index

About Us

The Mind of a Champion is a coaching organization located in Dallas, Texas. We provide "impact" sessions that introduce the concepts of Performance Intelligence. Our impact sessions consist of keynote presentations, workshops, and unique client and business development events. This only begins the training. We like to see lasting transformational change take hold with our clients. Those individuals and teams become fans of The Mind of a Champion when they apply the principle of Performance Intelligence and see the impact on results.

Just as in sports, training for real change is accomplished through spaced repetition—periodic reinforcement of the principles of Performance Intelligence. We provide spaced repetition through a number of methods, including individual coaching, team coaching, additional workshops, and our online Performance Training Center. Our clients find that these additional follow-up sessions maximize the training investment of the impact session. In fact, they find that these sessions maximize the investment they have made in training on the hard skills necessary for their profession as well. It is a double win—a win/win!

The Mind of a Champion's online Performance Training Center offers our community a wide variety of content and curriculum designed to augment the spaced repetition approach. The videos, audio streaming, articles, blogs, and user messages add another layer to spaced repetition. Because we desire true change in the thinking of our clients, we coach them to understand they have more game in them.

For more information on The Mind of a Champion, visit us online at: www.TheMindofaChampion.com.